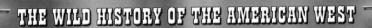

THE WILD HISTORY OF THE AMERICAN WEST

THE TRANSCONTINENTAL RAILROAD

AND THE GREAT RACE TO CONNECT THE NATION

Wim Coleman & Pat Perrin

MyReportLinks.com Books

an imprint of

 Enslow Publishers, Inc.

Box 398, 40 Industrial Road
Berkeley Heights, NJ 07922
USA

MyReportLinks.com Books, an imprint of Enslow Publishers, Inc. MyReportLinks®
is a registered trademark of Enslow Publishers, Inc.

Library of Congress Cataloging-in-Publication Data

Coleman, Wim.
  The transcontinental railroad and the great race to connect the nation / Wim Coleman & Pat Perrin.
     p. cm. — (The wild history of the American West)
  Includes bibliographical references and index.
  ISBN 1-59845-014-X
  1. Pacific railroads—Juvenile literature. [1. Railroads—History.] I. Perrin, Pat. II. Title. III. Series.
  TF25.P23.C65 2005
  385'.0979—dc22

                                    2005018610

Printed in the United States of America

10 9 8 7 6 5 4 3 2 1

To Our Readers:
Through the purchase of this book, you and your library gain access to the Report Links that specifically
back up this book.
The Publisher will provide access to the Report Links that back up this book and will keep these Report
Links up to date on **www.myreportlinks.com** for five years from the book's first publication date.
We have done our best to make sure all Internet addresses in this book were active and appropriate when
we went to press. However, the author and the Publisher have no control over, and assume no liability
for, the material available on those Internet sites or on other Web sites they may link to.
The usage of the MyReportLinks.com Books Web site is subject to the terms and conditions stated on the
Usage Policy Statement on **www.myreportlinks.com.**
A password may be required to access the Report Links that back up this book. The password is found
on the bottom of page 4 of this book.
Any comments or suggestions can be sent by e-mail to comments@myreportlinks.com or to the address
on the back cover.

Photo Credits: California State Railroad Museum Foundation, p. 54; © Corel Corporation, pp. 3, 27,
107, 109; © MMV BBC, p. 100; © 1995 PhotoDisc, Inc., pp. 19, 103; © 1995–2004 sfmuseum.org, p. 9;
© 1995–2005 Public Broadcasting Service, p. 11; © 1999 Oakland Museum of California, p. 74;
© 1999–2003 PBS Online/WGBH, p. 71; © 1999–2005 CPRR.org, pp. 29, 78; © 2000–05
LearnCalifornia.org, p. 69; © 2001 The West Film Project, p. 46; © J. Paul Getty Trust, p. 102; © 2004
Smithsonian Institution, pp. 65, 91; © 2005 CPRR.org, p. 66; © 2005 National Railroad Museum, p. 37;
© Union Pacific Railroad Corp. 1994–2005, p. 98; Enslow Publishers, Inc., p. 5; *Harper's Weekly*/Library
of Congress, pp. 76, 105; Library of Congress, pp. 7 (dog and man panning for gold, Indian chief), 13,
15, 17, 33, 35, 52, 56, 58, 94, 112; MyReportLinks.com Books, p. 4; National Archives, pp. 25, 48, 63,
72, 95; National Park Service, pp. 1, 7 (train), 23, 83, 96, 106, 111, 128; Photos.com, pp. 6, 7 (background, buffalo, wagon train); Reproduced from the *Dictionary of American Portraits*, published by Dover
Publications in 1967, pp. 82, 85, 86, 87, 88; © Stanford University, p. 92; The Rector and Visitors of the
University of Virginia, p. 44; U.S. Department of State, p. 21; U.S. Department of the Interior, p. 31.

Cover Photo: National Park Service

CONTENTS

MyReportLinks.com Books
Great Books, Great Links, Great for Research!

The Internet sites featured in this book can save you hours of research time. These Internet sites—we call them **"Report Links"**—are constantly changing, but we keep them up to date on our Web site.

When you see this "Approved Web Site" logo, you will know that we are directing you to a great Internet site that will help you with your research.

Give it a try! Type http://www.myreportlinks.com into your browser, click on the series title and enter the password, then click on the book title, and scroll down to the Report Links listed for this book.

The Report Links will bring you to great source documents, photographs, and illustrations. MyReportLinks.com Books save you time, feature Report Links that are kept up to date, and make report writing easier than ever! A complete listing of the Report Links can be found on pages 114–115 at the back of the book.

Please see "To Our Readers" on the copyright page for important information about this book, the MyReportLinks.com Web site, and the Report Links that back up this book.

Please enter WTR1434 if asked for a password.

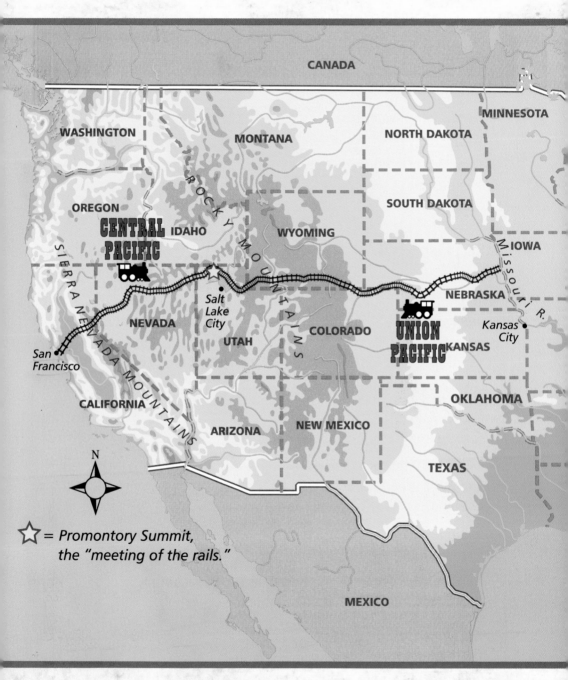

N

⭐ = *Promontory Summit,*
the "meeting of the rails."

▲ *The Transcontinental Railroad*

TRANSCONTINENTAL RAILROAD TIME LINE

▷ **1853**—Congress appropriates funds for explorations and surveys to find the best railway route from the Mississippi River to the Pacific Ocean.

▷ **1861**—*April:* The American Civil War begins, temporarily distracting people from plans to build a transcontinental railroad.

—*October:* Theodore Judah presents his surveys and maps to businessmen in California and politicians in Washington, D.C., demonstrating the solution to building a railroad across the Sierra Nevada Mountains.

—The Big Four—Charles Crocker, Collis P. Huntington, Mark Hopkins, and Leland Stanford—organize the Central Pacific Railroad Company to build a line from the West.

▷ **1862**—*July:* President Lincoln signs the Pacific Railroad Act. The act supports the Central Pacific Railroad Company and also charters the Union Pacific Railroad Company to build a line from the East.

▷ **1863**—*January 8:* The Central Pacific holds a groundbreaking ceremony.

—*October 26:* The Central Pacific begins laying railroad tracks from Sacramento, California.

—*October 30:* Thomas Clark Durant gains a controlling interest in the Union Pacific Railroad Company and becomes vice president of the company.

—*December 2:* The Union Pacific breaks ground in Omaha, Nebraska, to begin work on the eastern line.

▷ **1865**—*April 9:* The Civil War ends, releasing large numbers of men from service and making them available for other jobs.

—*April 14:* President Lincoln is assassinated.

—The Central Pacific begins hiring large numbers of Chinese workers, giving it the workforce it needs to build the line across the mountains.

—*July:* The Union Pacific starts laying track.

▷ **1866**—Central Pacific workers begin using nitroglycerine to blast tunnels through the mountains, speeding up their work considerably.

▷ **1868**—*June:* The first passenger train crosses the Sierra Nevada Mountains, from Sacramento, California, to Reno, Nevada.

▷ **1869**—*April:* Promontory Summit is selected as the meeting place for the eastern and western lines. Both companies race to lay the most track. In one remarkable effort, the Central Pacific workers lay 10 miles of track in one day.

—*May 10:* The Central Pacific and Union Pacific lines are joined in a ceremony at Promontory Summit in the Utah Territory.

—*May 15:* The first cross-country passenger train service begins.

◁ *Steam engines carried goods and people across the country.*

Chapter 1 ▶

DANGER IN THE HIGH SIERRAS

It was June 1861. High up in the Sierra Nevada Mountains of Northern California, two men on horseback stopped when one of them dismounted to tighten the girth strap on his horse's saddle. Suddenly, his big black horse broke away and

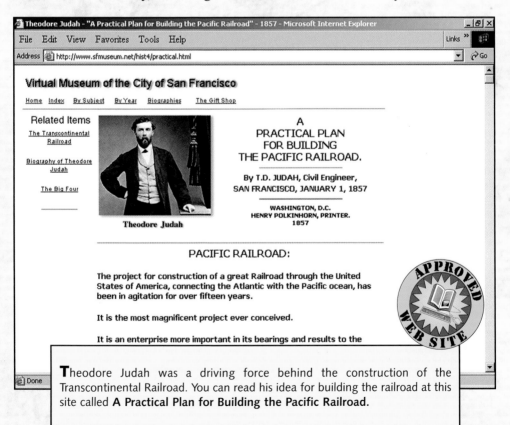

Theodore Judah – "A Practical Plan for Building the Pacific Railroad" – 1857 – Microsoft Internet Explorer

File   Edit   View   Favorites   Tools   Help   Links »

Address   http://www.sfmuseum.net/hist4/practical.html   ⟶ Go

Virtual Museum of the City of San Francisco

Home   Index   By Subject   By Year   Biographies   The Gift Shop

Related Items

The Transcontinental Railroad

Biography of Theodore Judah

The Big Four

Theodore Judah

A
PRACTICAL PLAN
FOR BUILDING
THE PACIFIC RAILROAD.

By T.D. JUDAH, Civil Engineer,
SAN FRANCISCO, JANUARY 1, 1857

WASHINGTON, D.C.
HENRY POLKINHORN, PRINTER.
1857

PACIFIC RAILROAD:

The project for construction of a great Railroad through the United States of America, connecting the Atlantic with the Pacific ocean, has been in agitation for over fifteen years.

It is the most magnificent project ever conceived.

It is an enterprise more important in its bearings and results to the

Theodore Judah was a driving force behind the construction of the Transcontinental Railroad. You can read his idea for building the railroad at this site called **A Practical Plan for Building the Pacific Railroad.**

charged wildly into the other rider's mount. That started the second horse dashing downhill, bucking and kicking. A stirrup broke, and the second horse's rider—Ted Judah—found himself flat on the ground.

Both horses jumped about while Judah lay helpless, their hooves striking the ground all around him. Judah expected one of the animals to land on top of him at any moment. The angry black horse that had started the trouble now seemed especially dangerous. Fortunately, both horses missed Judah with their hooves. As the horses galloped away toward the campground, the black horse kicked its saddle off, leaving pieces of it scattered along the trail.

Judah was left lying on the steep hillside, but he was not badly hurt. He and the other man—Doc Strong—walked back to the campground, carrying the pieces of the saddle. They decided to spend that afternoon retraining their horses.[1]

▶ Camping Out in Rough Country

Theodore Judah—sometimes called Crazy Judah—was up in those high mountains to carry out an unusual task. He was surveying a route for train tracks. He knew that if a train could cross the Sierra Nevadas, it would be possible to build a railroad across the entire country. Judah's persistence in that matter had earned him the nickname

"Crazy." In May, Judah had written to his wife, "I am running a line through the most difficult country ever conceived of for a Rail Road."[2]

Judah and the ten men in his corps of engineers were camped out in the wilderness. They were working above a 1,500-foot drop to the Bear River Gorge. The top of the mountain was 700 feet above their heads. Judah said that some slopes were so steep that "if you once slip it is all over."[3] Their new horses were still half wild, and their equipment was limited. Even during those summer months, they had to break the ice on their water buckets some mornings. Yet they were getting the job done.

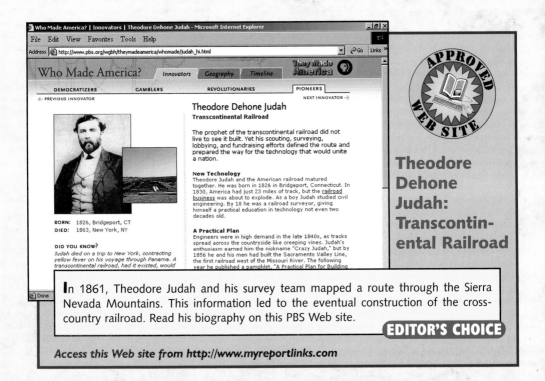

In 1861, Theodore Judah and his survey team mapped a route through the Sierra Nevada Mountains. This information led to the eventual construction of the cross-country railroad. Read his biography on this PBS Web site.

EDITOR'S CHOICE

Access this Web site from http://www.myreportlinks.com

Judah's survey team worked from sunrise to sunset. In the evening, four men plotted the measurements, drawing by lamplight and candlelight. Still, Judah wrote to his wife that he was quite comfortable in his tent, with its carpet of pine twigs and hay-filled mattress. On the center pole hung a lantern, saddle bags, and other items. He worked at a makeshift table—a drawing board set up on boxes—to write letters and make drawings.

When they had to work on very steep hillsides, the men used long ropes. A surveyor would tie one end of the rope around his waist and pass the rope around a tree. Another man held on to the other end, preventing the surveyor from falling very far. On such slopes, the work went very slowly. Some days, they were only able to survey one mile.

Ted Judah's wife, Anna, sometimes rode up the mountain to spend a few weeks with him. Anna Judah later wrote that because she "never held back" she was exactly the right wife for him.[4] Wearing long pantaloons (loose pants) instead of the skirts thought proper for women at that time, Anna Judah went out and enjoyed the incredible scenery. She pressed samples of the wildflowers that grew there and made sketches of the landscape. Some of her drawings were used on the original stock certificates of the Central Pacific Railroad Company.

Everybody in the surveying expedition knew how dangerous these mountains could be. Ted Judah and his party were not far from the pass where the Donner Party had become hopelessly trapped fifteen years earlier. Doc Strong, a storekeeper, was the one who led them there.

▷ The Donner Party Tragedy

By the time Judah was working in the Sierra Nevadas, the fate of the Donner Party was an often-told story. In the fall of 1846, a group of

△ This is railroad tunnel No. 41, built for the Transcontinental Railroad. Mt. Judah is in the background. Named for Ted Judah, this area is also known as Donner Pass.

families from Illinois and Iowa had tried to make their way through that mountain pass, on their way to California. Many of the travelers were members of the Donner family. Their entire journey had been hard, and they arrived at the pass later than they had planned. It was late October when the group paused at a lake—now called Donner Lake—to rest.

Heavy snows came early that year, surprising the Donner Party and trapping them in the pass. Their food ran out, the cold grew worse, and members of the party began to die. Some who remained alive were driven to cannibalism to survive. A small group of the party that eventually reached Sutter's Fort in northern California spurred several rescue attempts. By April, about half of the Donner Party was finally brought through to California. The rest had died in the pass or on the journey.

Newspapers all over the country printed letters and diaries written by members of the Donner Party. Some stories grew wilder as they were told and retold. That route through the mountains was almost completely abandoned, and emigration to California in general fell off. In 1848, when President James K. Polk (1845–49) announced the discovery of gold in California, large numbers of people began to rush to the Far West. The "Donner Pass" came back into widespread use because it was the shortest route to the gold fields near Sutter's Fort.[5]

In spite of the famous Donner Party tragedy, Ted Judah became convinced that he had found the best place to build a railroad across the Sierra Nevada mountains.

▶ Why Here?

The Sierra Nevada Mountains reach over 7,000 feet high. In most areas, the mountains have a double summit. That means you cross one mountaintop, go down into a valley, and then have to climb again to cross another mountain. The Donner Pass was different, as historian Wendell Huffman explained on PBS (Public Broadcasting

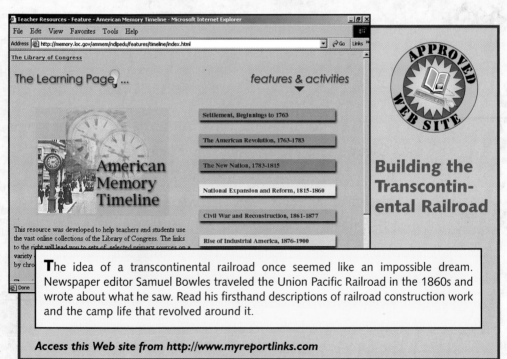

Building the Transcontinental Railroad

The idea of a transcontinental railroad once seemed like an impossible dream. Newspaper editor Samuel Bowles traveled the Union Pacific Railroad in the 1860s and wrote about what he saw. Read his firsthand descriptions of railroad construction work and the camp life that revolved around it.

Access this Web site from http://www.myreportlinks.com

Service). "At Donner, you've only got one summit. You come up the American River, you go down the Truckee River. And by being on the ridge above the river, you have a nice continuous plain . . . that you use as a ramp."[6]

As dangerous as the Donner Pass was, trains could use that route. Ted Judah was right. At great risk to his own life, he had found a way across the Sierra Nevada Mountains.

Judah was a well-trained engineer, and he also had the gift of persuasion. He was able to convince investors and government officials that a railroad could actually get across those mountains. Crazy Judah had solved the great problem that had always before blocked plans for a transcontinental railroad.

Earlier Dreamers

In the early 1800s, steam engines were in use in Great Britain to haul coal cars. Although not one was yet in use in America, an engineer named Robert Mills believed they should be. Mills proposed that a steam-driven carriage on rails could run from the Mississippi River Valley into the Northwest's Columbia River Valley. Mills may have been the first professional architect born in America (in 1781), and he would later design the Washington Monument. His notions about transportation, though, were ignored.

In 1830, eastern railroad entrepreneur William C. Redfield promoted the idea of a train line to the West. He published a pamphlet suggesting that money formerly wasted on wars—such as the War of 1812 with Great Britain—could be better spent on a project to benefit the nation. Redfield proposed that a "Great Railway" be built from the Atlantic states to the Mississippi Valley, and even across the entire country. Like Mills, Redfield was widely ignored.

During the following years, citizens of various communities began to take an interest in the possibility of a transcontinental railroad. In each case, they pleaded the case to have the line run

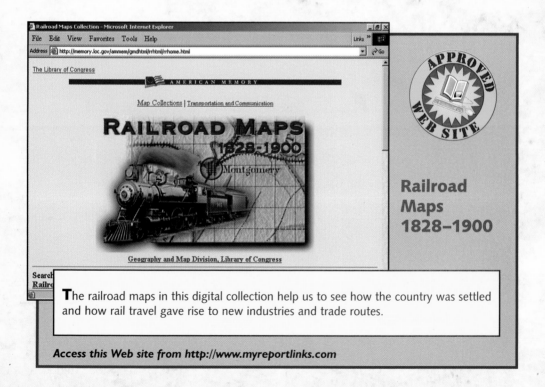

Railroad Maps 1828–1900

The railroad maps in this digital collection help us to see how the country was settled and how rail travel gave rise to new industries and trade routes.

Access this Web site from http://www.myreportlinks.com

through their own towns, bringing new trade, business opportunities, and prosperity.

Some creative thinkers saw the railroad as a link in a new trade route. They expected to send goods to the West Coast by train, to be shipped from there to China, India, and other nations on the far side of the Pacific Ocean. They imagined the silks of the Orient brought directly to American shops—even though many of those dreamers had no experience at all with Asian nations or even with international trade. However, one of those early dreamers, a merchant named Asa Whitney, did have those experiences.

▶ Asa Whitney

Whitney was a distant cousin of famous inventor Eli Whitney.[7] In the 1820s and 1830s, Asa Whitney traveled to Europe to buy items for import to the United States. In Great Britain, he experienced the newest thing in transportation technology— he took a ride on a train. British steam locomotives sped along at up to 40 miles per hour, and Whitney was quick to recognize their potential. He reported to the U.S. Senate that, "We could have a more ready, frequent, and cheap communication than the present long and dangerous voyage around either of the capes."[8]

In 1842, Whitney's business ventures floundered and he found himself in debt. He decided to delve into a new opportunity that was just developing—trade with China. His trip to China was long, uncomfortable, and unpleasant. The ship had to sail southeast across the Atlantic, around the Cape of Good Hope at the tip of Africa, then northward to the China Sea. It took 153 days. Along the way, Whitney was horrified by

Building a railroad through the Sierra Nevada Mountains in the 1800s would be no easy task. As the Donner Party found out, the heavy snowfall and huge snowdrifts can make the mountains nearly impassable. Now, modern roads weave through the Sierra Nevadas.

the conditions under which people from poorer countries lived and worked.

Whitney spent a year in China, arranging to export teas, spices, and other goods to the United States. By the time he returned to the United States in 1844, he was wealthy from his business ventures and eager to devote his life to the good of humankind.[9] During the tedious return trip, he began to dwell on the idea of a transcontinental railroad.

Whitney believed a great coast-to-coast railroad would place America at the center of trade between Europe and Asia. He also thought that connecting the people of the world would bring "all our immensely wide-spread population together as one vast city; the moral and social effects of which must harmonize all together as one family, with but one interest—the general good of all."[10] As Asa Whitney envisioned it, all the world would join the American family.

Unable to arouse any enthusiasm in Congress, Whitney spent the next six years publicizing his ideas. Although he attracted some public interest, Congress remained skeptical. Senator Thomas Hart Benton of Missouri deemed the idea impossible, telling Whitney, "You are one hundred years before the time."[11] However, Benton also remarked that if there was ever such a railroad, it should start in St. Louis.

Whitney did not succeed in spurring Congress into action at that time, but he planted the idea in the popular imagination. Asa Whitney died in 1872, shortly after the Transcontinental Railroad was completed.

The Western Wilderness

All of those early dreamers faced a general belief that most of the West was useless and dangerous. The United States of America was located to the east of the Missouri River. Some leaders believed that was as far as the nation could or should ever reach. Before 1840, few settlers went beyond the Mississippi River.[12] According to one United States

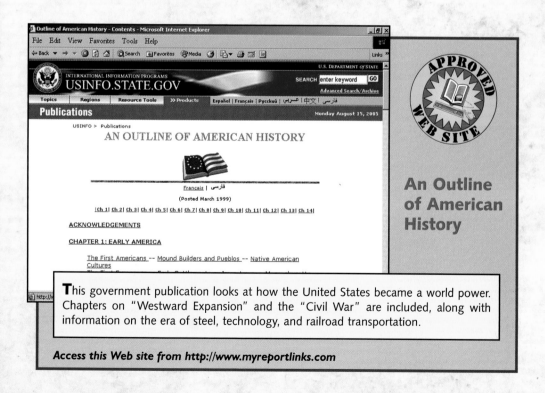

An Outline of American History

This government publication looks at how the United States became a world power. Chapters on "Westward Expansion" and the "Civil War" are included, along with information on the era of steel, technology, and railroad transportation.

Access this Web site from http://www.myreportlinks.com

senator, the West was a place "which no American citizen should be compelled to inhabit unless as a punishment for crime."[13]

Even so, some American leaders had always understood that the nation would expand. In 1803, President Thomas Jefferson wrote in a letter to the governor of Virginia, James Monroe:

> It is impossible not to look forward to distant times, when our rapid multiplication will expand itself beyond those limits and cover the whole northern, if not the southern, continent, with a people speaking the same language, governed in similar forms and by similar laws . . .[14]

That year, Jefferson seized the opportunity to buy the Louisiana Territory—more than doubling the size of the United States—without knowing much about what that territory was like. In 1804 the president put Meriwether Lewis and William Clark at the head of a western expedition called the Corps of Discovery. Lewis and Clark hoped to find a water route across the country, which would provide an easier way to travel than land routes.

There was no water route across North America, and cross-country travel by land remained difficult and dangerous. But eventually, Theodore Judah would also go searching for a route to the West—this time for a way to get there by train. And Judah would find exactly what he was looking for.

Chapter 2 ▶

SEEING THE POSSIBILITIES

In December 1845, President James K. Polk advised Congress that the United States should expand west. "The people of this continent alone have the right to decide their own destiny," he said.[1] Although Polk did not mention it, much of the West actually belonged to Mexico, and

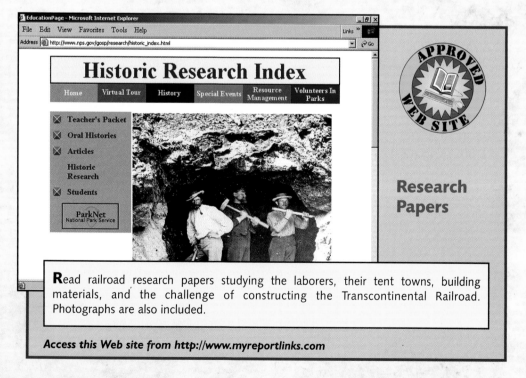

EducationPage - Microsoft Internet Explorer

File   Edit   View   Favorites   Tools   Help   Links »

Address http://www.nps.gov/gosp/research/historic_index.html

Historic Research Index

| Home | Virtual Tour | History | Special Events | Resource Management | Volunteers In Parks |

- ☒ Teacher's Packet
- ☒ Oral Histories
- ☒ Articles
- Historic Research
- ☒ Students

ParkNet
National Park Service

Research Papers

Read railroad research papers studying the laborers, their tent towns, building materials, and the challenge of constructing the Transcontinental Railroad. Photographs are also included.

Access this Web site from http://www.myreportlinks.com

the northwest boundary between the United States and Canada had not yet been officially determined.

Manifest Destiny

That same month, New York newspaper journalist John O'Sullivan wrote that it was "the nation's manifest destiny to overspread and to possess the whole of the continent which Providence has given us . . . "[2]

The term "Manifest Destiny" quickly became popular with Americans—it gave them a sense of purpose, even of divine mission. The Public Broadcasting System's online companion to "The U.S.–Mexican War (1846–48)" explains it this way:

> The people of the United States felt it was their mission to extend the "boundaries of freedom" to others by imparting their idealism and belief in democratic institutions to those who were capable of self-government. It excluded those people who were perceived as being incapable of self-government, such as American Indian people and those of non-European origin.[3]

There were also very practical reasons for Americans to start moving westward. Due to high birth rates and immigration, the population of the United States had grown from more than 5 million in 1800 to more than 23 million by mid-century.[4] Land on the frontier was cheap; sometimes it was even free. Owning land meant independence. and opportunities for new business ventures. Landowning families could become self-sufficient, possibly even wealthy.

As the people of America became convinced that their nation was destined to control the continent, they also began thinking about travel. How might one more quickly and easily get to those outer reaches of the nation?

▶ Getting There by Land

At that time, the area west of the Mississippi River that is commonly called the Great Plains was then known as the Great American Desert. Most explorers who had ventured across it had reported it to

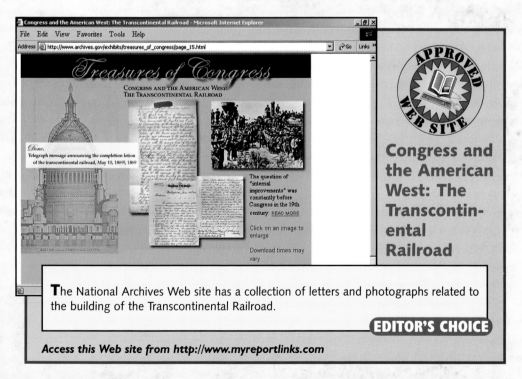

Congress and the American West: The Transcontinental Railroad

The National Archives Web site has a collection of letters and photographs related to the building of the Transcontinental Railroad.

EDITOR'S CHOICE

Access this Web site from http://www.myreportlinks.com

be barren. Explorers who spotted sand dunes and desert areas thought the whole western half of the country must be the same. Even when Oregon and northern California were found to offer green pastures, the center of the country was still considered a wasteland.

When settlers got a better look at the land they were crossing, they realized that the Great Plains also offered good grazing and possibilities for farming. They realized that the Midwest was not entirely desert, after all, and so travelers soon began to populate those areas along the way.

The most practical cross-country land route was the Oregon Trail. The trail reached from Independence, Missouri, to Oregon City, Oregon, with branches southward to California. The leg of the trail that extended to California was often referred to as the California Trail. These trails could be traveled on foot, on mule or horseback, or by wagon. The trip was over 2,000 miles, and it took about six months by covered wagon.

▶ Covered Wagons

Covered wagons were uncomfortable and unsafe. They did not have springs to make the ride more comfortable. They did not have brakes for stopping. Wagons were usually pulled by slow moving oxen, which were sturdier and more dependable than horses. Even those who had wagons generally

▲ *For many, driving a covered wagon along the Oregon and California Trail was the most inexpensive way to make their way west. These wagons are rolling over what was once part of the Oregon Trail.*

walked the entire distance, sometimes barefoot. The wagons carried household goods and those people who needed to ride in them—children, the elderly, and the sick.

Sometimes a wagon would fail to make it across a river or would slide off the edge of a cliff.

Sometimes the animals pulling a wagon became weak, or even collapsed. Then the family usually had to abandon their belongings, and they would count themselves fortunate if no lives were lost. Many groups had to turn back or end their journey before reaching their goal.

One person in ten died on the way, most often of cholera, other diseases spread by poor sanitation, or accidental gunshots.[5] In some areas, American Indian tribes were dangerous to the travelers, though other tribes were quite helpful.

Improvements in Land Transportation

In the 1850s and 1860s, a newer means of transportation delivered mail and people between Missouri and California—the stagecoach. Although stagecoaches cut the travel time down considerably, they were expensive and often uncomfortable. The coaches traveled about eight miles per hour and had to stop to change horses every twelve or fifteen miles.[6] As many as twenty passengers might be crammed into one coach—where they breathed dust and suffered from the heat or cold.

In 1862, author Mark Twain rode a stagecoach from St. Joseph, Missouri, to Carson City, Nevada. That trip, which took fifteen to seventeen days, cost $150 (more than $3,000 in today's dollars).[7] In his book *Roughing It,* Twain calls the coach "a swinging and swaying cage" in which passengers were tossed about along with the mail bags.[8] The following paragraph is from Twain's description of his stagecoach ride:

> We began to get into country, now, threaded here and there with little streams. These had high, steep banks on each side, and every time we flew down one bank and scrambled up the other, our party inside got mixed somewhat. First we would all lie down in a pile at the forward end of the stage, nearly in a sitting posture, and in a second we would shoot to the other end and stand on

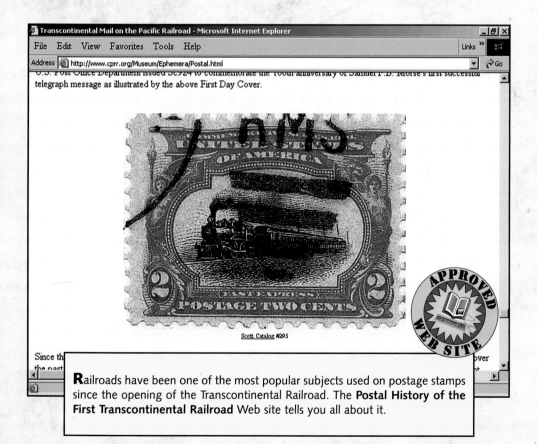

telegraph message as illustrated by the above First Day Cover.

Scott Catalog #295

Railroads have been one of the most popular subjects used on postage stamps since the opening of the Transcontinental Railroad. The **Postal History of the First Transcontinental Railroad** Web site tells you all about it.

our heads. And we would sprawl and kick, too, and ward off ends and corners of mail-bags that came lumbering over us and about us; and as the dust rose from the tumult, we would all sneeze in chorus, and the majority of us would grumble, and probably say some hasty thing, like: "Take your elbow out of my ribs! Can't you quit crowding?"[9]

Getting There by Water

Some travelers chose to go to California by water. The quickest way was to take a ship down the Atlantic Coast, cross overland at the Isthmus of Panama, and take another ship north to San Francisco. Human porters and mules carried goods about fifty miles across the isthmus. People rode mules or hiked through the jungle on foot. They had to contend with snakes, poisonous insects, jungle beasts such as jaguars and pumas, bandits, and sometimes heavy rains. They were also in constant danger from diseases such as yellow fever, malaria, and cholera.

The longer sea route—around Cape Horn at the tip of South America—was also dangerous. Gigantic waves and gale-force winds challenged even the most able seaman. The 13,600-mile trip around the Horn was expensive and took two to five months. Even so, in good weather the trip around the Horn might be easier on travelers who could afford it than the overland route.

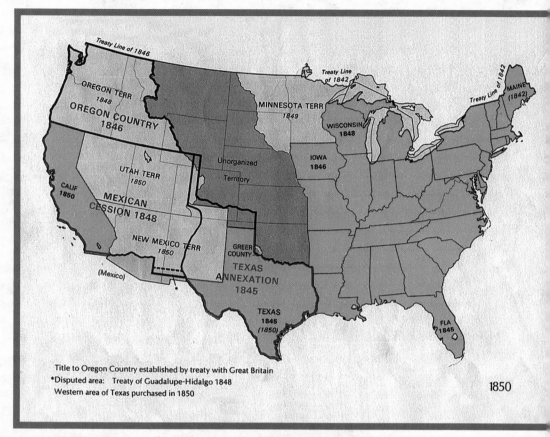

Title to Oregon Country established by treaty with Great Britain
*Disputed area: Treaty of Guadalupe-Hidalgo 1848
Western area of Texas purchased in 1850

1850

△ This map shows how the United States had expanded by 1850, after the conclusion of the Mexican-American War.

▶ All at Once . . .

By 1845, Texas had become independent of Mexico. California and much of the Southwest were part of Mexico. Ownership of the Oregon Territory was still in dispute with the British, who controlled Canada. Almost all of the United States population was clustered on the eastern edge of the country.

Then things began to happen—some of them at nearly the same time. In 1845, the United States annexed Texas, which became the twenty-eighth state. In 1846, a treaty with Great Britain granted the Oregon Territory to the United States. From 1846 to 1848, the United States and Mexico fought the Mexican-American War over the issue of boundaries. The United States won that war, gaining California and the entire Southwest. The nation then reached from the Atlantic to the Pacific Ocean. Its north and south boundaries were about where they are today.

▷ The Gold Rush

In 1848, nine days after the war with Mexico ended, gold was discovered at Sutter's Mill in northern California. President Polk was anxious to get people to move westward, so he announced the discovery to the public. Those who hurried to get to California for gold were referred to as "forty-niners." The 1849 Gold Rush helped to populate California, and in 1850 the territory became a state.

After that, migration to California varied from year to year. In *Nothing Like It in the World,* historian Stephen Ambrose comments on the fortune seekers:

The forty-niners, who came before statistics keepers from the government appeared to count them,

Some went to California by sailing around the tip of South America. Or, sometimes people would stop in Panama, cross the narrow strip of land called the Isthmus of Panama, and sail the rest of the way. As this cartoon shows, these ships were often crowded and it was expensive to get a spot.

were followed by more fortune seekers some years, less in others. In 1850, a record 55,000 emigrants, nearly all male, headed west from the Missouri bound for California. About 5,000 died from a cholera epidemic, so the next year the emigration count was down to 10,000. But by 1852, it was back up to 50,000. By 1860, more then 300,000 . . . had made the overland journey.[10]

Meanwhile, United States Railroads Race Along

Steam locomotives had been pulling trains in England since the 1820s. But in the United States at that time, railway cars were pulled by horses. These horse-drawn railway cars were first used to haul minerals from mines in Massachusetts and Pennsylvania. In 1828, building began on tracks for the Baltimore and Ohio Rail Road Company, the first United States commercial line for carrying freight and passengers. The rails were made of wood, and the cars were horse drawn.

The existing steam locomotives of the time had not proved to be practical on American tracks. Heavy British locomotives were built for the flat, straight tracks used in England. They tended to jump off the tracks when they tried to go around the tight curves that rail lines in the United States had to follow. Stagecoaches were still the best transportation available between major cities such as New York and Philadelphia.

As usual, some people thought that was how things would always be. Others—such as Peter Cooper—were better at seeing the possibilities.

Peter Cooper and Tom Thumb

Peter Cooper was the founder of The Cooper Union for the Advancement of Science and Art in New York City. He was sure that steam-powered trains could transport passengers and freight in the United States, as they did in England. He decided to design and build his own steam locomotive in a size that could make the turns on American tracks. As Cooper later explained in the *Boston Herald,* he had to make some parts and scrounge for others.

> I got some boiler iron and made a boiler about as big as an ordinary washboiler, and then how to connect the boiler with the engine I didn't know. . . . I couldn't find any iron pipes. . . . So I took two muskets and broke off the wood part and used the barrels for tubing to the boiler. . . . I went into a coachmaker's shop and made the locomotive,

▲ An image of Tom Thumb while the classic train was on display at the 1939 World's Fair. Peter Cooper built the Tom Thumb in 1830, and it was the first steam train that could work on American tracks.

which I called the *Tom Thumb* because it was so insignificant.[11]

▷ The Race

In August 1830, Cooper impressed a group of dignitaries by taking them on a short train ride. Then he was challenged by a group of stagecoach owners to race *Tom Thumb* against a horse-drawn carriage. Cooper accepted the challenge. Here is how one witness described the race:

> A gallant horse of great beauty and power was driven . . . from town attached to another car on the second track. . . . The start being even, away went horse and engine, the snort of the one and the puff of the other keeping time and time. At first the horse had the best of it. . . . The horse was perhaps a quarter of a mile ahead, when the safety-valve of the engine lifted and the thin blue vapor issuing from it showed an excess of steam. The blower whistled, the steam blew off in vapory clouds, the pace increased, the passengers shouted, the engine gained on the horse. Soon it lapped him . . . the race was neck and neck, nose and nose. Then the engine passed the horse, and a great hurrah hailed the victory. But . . . just at this time, when the gray's master was about giving up, the band which drove the pulley which moved the blower, slipped from the driver, the safety-valve ceased to scream, and the engine for want of breath began to wheeze and pant. . . . The horse gained on the machine and passed it.[12]

The horse-drawn carriage won the race, but the little locomotive had proved its practicality.[13] By the 1840s, people and goods were traveling between major cities by train. The "iron horse" was replacing real horses for journeys of any distance, but there was still no way to take a train from one side of the country to the other.

The World's First Transcontinental Railroad

When the rush for California gold began, traffic across the Isthmus of Panama suddenly increased. In 1850, work started on an American-financed rail line across the swamps, jungles, and mountains of the isthmus. When only 7 miles of track

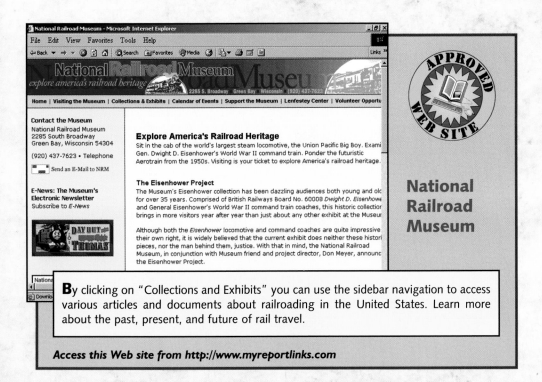

By clicking on "Collections and Exhibits" you can use the sidebar navigation to access various articles and documents about railroading in the United States. Learn more about the past, present, and future of rail travel.

Access this Web site from http://www.myreportlinks.com

had been laid, the Panama Railway had already started making money. The fare for the 7-mile train ride was twenty-five dollars per person. Just to walk the rest of the way along the railroad's right-of-way cost seven dollars per person. In spite of the high prices, those eager to prospect for gold just kept coming. On both the Atlantic and the Pacific, steamship lines began regular runs to get travelers to and from the isthmus.

The 48-mile railroad line was completed in 1855. Crossing between the Atlantic and Pacific oceans, the Panama Railway was the world's first transcontinental railroad.

▶ Thinking Bigger

During the 1850s, railroad lines stretched across every one of the American states east of the Mississippi River. By 1860, there would be more than 30,000 miles of track.[14] Excitement was building for a grand venture—a transcontinental railroad across the United States. Such a railroad would make it easier for settlers to populate the West. It would move mail and goods across the country. And it would help protect the sprawling nation by providing a way to move American troops quickly to areas beyond the Mississippi.

In 1853, Congress appropriated $150,000 for explorations and surveys to find the best railway route from the Mississippi River to the Pacific

Ocean. Those surveyors marked out five possible routes across the Midwest. They also reported favorably on the land and climate in the Great Plains. They said that midwestern land was rich with minerals and suitable for farming. Some who had feared to enter what they had thought of as the Great American Desert were encouraged to move westward.

In spite of the surveyors' hard work and good news, disputes raged about the railroad's possible route. Those arguments often had little to do with surveys.

Chapter 3 ▶

GETTING STARTED, 1860—1863

When it came to the question of where any railroad might be built, there were lots of things to disagree about. For example, there was the issue of bridges. In 1857, the Rock Island Bridge Company built the first railroad bridge across the Mississippi River. When a steamboat crashed into the bridge, the boat caught fire and burned. The angry boat owner promptly sued the bridge builders.[1]

Those who supported the boat owner argued that nothing should be allowed to get in the way of river navigation. A little-known lawyer named Abraham Lincoln argued for the railroad's right to build bridges across rivers. Lincoln investigated the incident and reported that the steamboat crash had been caused by pilot error.

Lincoln also told the jury how important railroads were to the nation's economic future. He pointed out that traveling east and west was just as important as traveling north and south along the river. The jury could not reach a decision, and the case was dismissed. Railroads could go ahead and build bridges—without which, the Transcontinental Railroad could never have existed.

The Issue of Slavery

Slavery caused many problems in the expanding United States. Every time a new territory was organized, Congress debated whether or not slavery would be allowed there. Through the years, compromises were made. Some territories were allowed to make their own decisions about slavery. But whenever a territory became a state, the citizens elected members to the Senate and House of Representatives. Each side, pro slavery and antislavery, was determined that the other not gain a majority in Congress.

In 1820, the Missouri Compromise kept the existing balance of power between the two sides. Missouri would be allowed to join the Union as a slaveholding state if Maine could join as a non-slaveholding state. The Missouri Compromise also outlawed slavery in the northern half of the Louisiana Purchase—the part that had not yet become states.

In the 1850s, the issue of slavery affected plans for the Transcontinental Railroad. Wherever railroads were built, communities prospered. They gained people, jobs, and income. Political leaders were all eager for the proposed railroad to go through their own areas. Sometimes they were just as determined to keep the railroad out of other areas.

Northern states were not willing to build a line that would start in the South and help the Southern states grow stronger. They also feared that such a railroad would help spread the practice of slavery.

Southerners wanted the railroad to start in their area, and would not back a northern route. They had strong support from President Franklin Pierce's secretary of war, Jefferson Davis. (Pierce was president from 1853 to 1857.) Davis gave the railway survey teams their instructions and oversaw their progress. He recommended that the Transcontinental Railroad start in Louisiana and follow a southern route to California.

▶ Senator Douglas and Attorney Lincoln

Illinois senator Stephen A. Douglas was among those who early on supported the idea of a railroad across the country. He was set on making Chicago the eastern end of the line. If the Kansas and Nebraska territories became states, they would be likely to support his plan in Congress. But Douglas would also need the backing of Southern senators.

In 1854, Senator Douglas introduced the Kansas-Nebraska Act, which repealed the Missouri

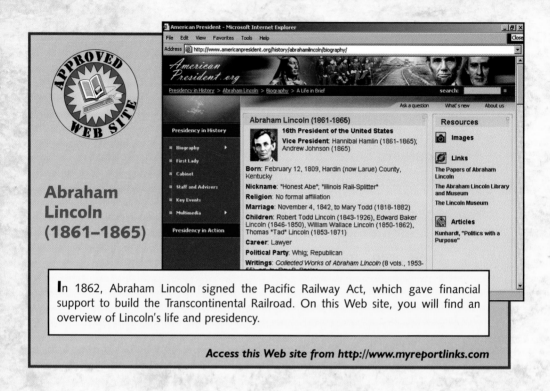

Abraham
Lincoln
(1861–1865)

In 1862, Abraham Lincoln signed the Pacific Railway Act, which gave financial support to build the Transcontinental Railroad. On this Web site, you will find an overview of Lincoln's life and presidency.

Access this Web site from http://www.myreportlinks.com

Compromise.[2] The act allowed territories to choose for themselves whether or not to allow slavery. It passed in Congress, and President Pierce signed it. Then both Southerners and Northerners rushed into Kansas and fought to control the territory. The struggle became violent; it earned the nickname "Bleeding Kansas."

Another citizen of Illinois objected to the repeal of the Missouri Compromise. Attorney Abraham Lincoln spoke out against the act, and against the immorality of slavery itself. He soon attracted a following of activists who were also against the expansion of slavery in the United States.

In 1858, Lincoln made a bid for the Senate seat held by Douglas, and the two men held a series of public debates. According to Lincoln, whether or not blacks and whites were equals, the Declaration of Independence guaranteed everyone the same rights. Douglas completely rejected that idea. Lincoln demanded that slavery not be allowed to expand beyond the South. Douglas hoped that letting each area make its own choice would allow a peaceful end to the arguments.

Douglas held onto his senate seat, but the debates made Lincoln famous. In 1860, Lincoln beat Douglas in the race for United States president. After Lincoln's election, Southern states began seceding from the Union. In April 1861, Confederates fired on the Union's Fort Sumter in South Carolina. The American Civil War had begun. Jefferson Davis was made president of the Confederate States of America, while Lincoln remained president of the Union.

▷ Theodore Judah and the Big Four

As the Civil War was getting started, Ted Judah was up in the Sierra Nevada Mountains, struggling with steep slopes and half-trained horses. Judah's surveying expedition had been financially supported by a group of four Sacramento, California, businessmen.

File Edit View Favorites Tools Help

Address http://www.pbs.org/weta/thewest/people/s_z/stanford.htm   Go   Links »

NEW PERSPECTIVES ON **THE WEST**

THE PROGRAM   PEOPLE   PLACES   EVENTS   RESOURCES   LESSON PLANS   QUIZ

PEOPLE

A-C

D-H

I-R

S-Z

Sacagawea

Santa Anna, Antonio
López de

Seguin, Juan

Serra, Father
Junipero

Sheridan, Philip

Sherm...

Te...

S...

S...

Sutt...

Tatank...
(Sitting...

Terry, A...

Leland Stanford

(1824-1893)

One of the "Big Four" who built California's Central Pacific railroad, Leland Stanford brought a sweeping political influence to the partnership that insured this privately financed project all the advantages of public funding.

Stanford was born into a well-off farming family in Watervliet, New York. After a superb secondary education and several years of higher education, Stanford entered an elite law office to prepare for a career as an attorney, passing his bar exam in 1848. He soon moved to Wisconsin, where he began to practice his profession.

After three years in Wisconsin, Stanford and his new wife decided to move to California, where several of his brothers had already found success as merchants. Stanford joined them in 1852 and soon began making enormous sums of money by selling equipment to miners in northern California. He also became involved in politics, first as a justice of the peace, then as the unsuccessful 1857 Republican candidate for state treasurer, and in 1859 as the unsuccessful Republican gubernatorial candidate. Stanford was finally elected...

Leland Stanford was one of the "Big Four" that planned the Central Pacific Railroad. He acted as the president of Central Pacific until his death in 1893. This biography is part of the PBS series and Web site called **New Perspectives on the West.**

Charles Crocker ran a dry-goods store and was a member of the state legislature. Collis P. Huntington and Mark Hopkins were partners in a general store. Another storekeeper, Leland Stanford, was elected governor of California in September 1861. They all became partners in the Central Pacific Railroad project. Ted Judah and Doc Strong, who was working on the mountain with Judah, were also partners in the business venture.

That September, Judah and Strong brought the other partners their surveys and maps. Judah described the tunnels and bridges that would have to be built. He convinced his partners that it could be done. The pleased businessmen decided to send Judah to Washington to convince Congress to support the project with land and money. Judah traveled east by way of the Isthmus of Panama, his preferred route.

In October 1861, Ted Judah arrived in the nation's capital, carrying his maps and measurements, along with Anna Judah's paintings and drawings. However, it was very hard to get the attention of congressmen who were busy raising and equipping an army. President Lincoln still strongly supported the idea of a transcontinental railroad. But Lincoln also had the Civil War to worry about.

The Railroad War

Some historians consider the Civil War to be the first modern war. New technologies—such as ironclad ships, submarines, observation balloons, railroads, new artillery weapons, and telegraph communications—were used by both sides. Some refer to the conflict as the "Railroad War" because of the major role that trains played.

When the Civil War began, the North had about twenty thousand miles of railroad track. The South had less than half as much. The Union army used their widespread rail service to

▲ Rail transportation was very important during the Civil War. Both the Union and Confederate armies spent a good deal of time trying to sabotage the other side's tracks.

transport troops and supplies wherever they were needed. Each side sabotaged the other's trains and telegraph lines whenever they could. The Confederate army destroyed more track than the Union army. However, because the North had much more track than the South, the Union army destroyed a higher percentage of track.

The Great Locomotive Chase

In one famous Civil War raid, a stolen locomotive was chased down by another one on the same track.[3] In the spring of 1862, Union troops led by a spy named James Andrews slipped into Georgia. They planned to take an engine and flee to the North, destroying railroad tracks, bridges, and telegraph lines as they went. Disguised as civilians, Andrews's raiders traveled as ordinary passengers on a Southern train. The train carried the twenty Union raiders into a Confederate army camp. The story was related by one of the survivors, William Pittenger:

> It was a foggy, rainy day. When the train stopped, the engineer, conductor, and passengers went to breakfast. Andrews's raiders went into action. They uncoupled the locomotive, tender, and three empty baggage cars from the rest of the train. They all got on board, fired up the locomotive, and "the little train darted away, leaving the camp and the station in the wildest uproar. . . ."[4]

At first, the raid seemed to be succeeding. The raiders talked their way past Confederate stations, claiming to be Southerners running a weapons train. They tore up track behind them, gathering up railroad ties to be used for fuel. They cut telegraph lines.

But Southern troops were soon after the thieves. The Confederate conductor and a machine shop foreman ran after the stolen train on foot. Then they grabbed a handcar and pumped their way to another Confederate locomotive on a good sidetrack. Loaded with soldiers, the second engine caught up with the raiders. It followed close behind the stolen train, trying to keep the Union soldiers from damaging the tracks or the telegraph line.

The Pace Quickens

Both engines raced along at top speed. Andrews's raiders dropped off cars to block their pursuers. But the Confederates overcame all obstacles and quickly got back into shooting range. Every time they passed a station, the raiders cut the telegraph line, so no warning could be sent ahead. They wanted to stop and burn a bridge, but the rain made it hard to start a fire, and their pursuers were still very close behind. Pittenger wrote that every time they thought they had lost the Southern pursuers, "the smoke was again seen, and the shrill whistle was like the scream of a bird of prey."[5]

Finally, the stolen engine ran out of fuel. The Union soldiers had to leap from the locomotive and scatter into the woods. Many were captured, and some of them were hung. Others escaped from prison and made their way back home.

Great Plains and Great Trains

In spite of the war, President Lincoln gave as much attention as he could to westward expansion. In 1862 he signed the Homestead Act, which gave settlers 160 acres of public land free if they lived there for five years. He also pushed for a bill to support the Transcontinental Railroad. Lincoln realized the importance of keeping the western part of the country connected with the East. He wanted to make sure the western states allied with the North. So in June 1862, even as the war roared on, Congress passed the Pacific Railroad Act and Lincoln signed it.

Two railroad companies were authorized to build a railroad line across the continent. The Union Pacific would build westward across the Great Plains. The Central Pacific would start in Sacramento, California, and build eastward through the Sierra Nevada. In addition to grants of land, the companies would be paid according to how much track they laid. At that time, no one

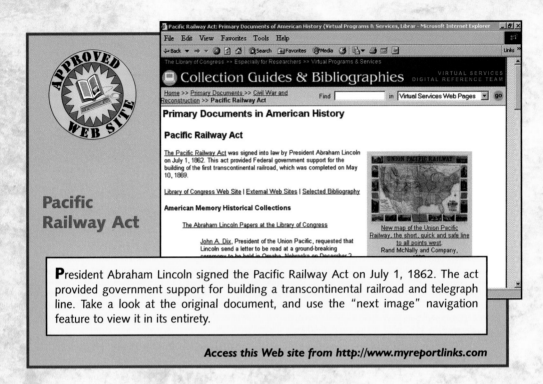

Primary Documents in American History

Pacific Railway Act

The Pacific Railway Act was signed into law by President Abraham Lincoln on July 1, 1862. This act provided Federal government support for the building of the first transcontinental railroad, which was completed on May 10, 1869.

Library of Congress Web Site | External Web Sites | Selected Bibliography

American Memory Historical Collections

The Abraham Lincoln Papers at the Library of Congress

John A. Dix, President of the Union Pacific, requested that Lincoln send a letter to be read at a ground-breaking ceremony to be held in Omaha, Nebraska on December 2,

New map of the Union Pacific Railway, the short, quick and safe line to all points west. Rand McNally and Company,

President Abraham Lincoln signed the Pacific Railway Act on July 1, 1862. The act provided government support for building a transcontinental railroad and telegraph line. Take a look at the original document, and use the "next image" navigation feature to view it in its entirety.

Access this Web site from http://www.myreportlinks.com

thought to specify where the two lines would meet—or even the town where the eastern section would begin.

The Pacific Railroad Act also called for a telegraph line to be built. Telegraph workers were to set up their poles and string cable alongside the railroad, connecting populated areas as they went.

▶ **The Ultimatum**

While Ted Judah was in the East lobbying Congress to support the railroad, the California businessmen got organized. With grand speeches and celebrations, they broke ground for the project in downtown Sacramento on January 8, 1863.

Leland Stanford, a partner as well as the California governor, dug the first shovelful of dirt. They put Charles Crocker in charge of building the railroad.

When Judah returned, he was upset by what he found. The partners were not paying their workers on time, and they were changing decisions Judah had made. Even worse, Judah did not trust Crocker, who was in charge of the construction. Judah was almost certain that the "Big Four" businessmen were misusing public money. And Judah was disappointed that no track had been laid. Doc Strong was the only one who would take Judah's side, and the disagreements among the group grew worse by the week.

A Fateful Journey

Finally, in the summer of 1863, the Big Four gave Judah an ultimatum—either buy us out or we will buy you out. The businessmen and politicians were shutting out the dreamer who made the whole thing happen.

Ted Judah and his wife, Anna, headed east, where they thought they could find backers to help them buy the other partners out. But this time, crossing the Isthmus of Panama, Ted Judah fell ill. He had caught one of the deadly diseases— scholars are unsure whether it was yellow fever or typhoid—that always threatened travelers on that

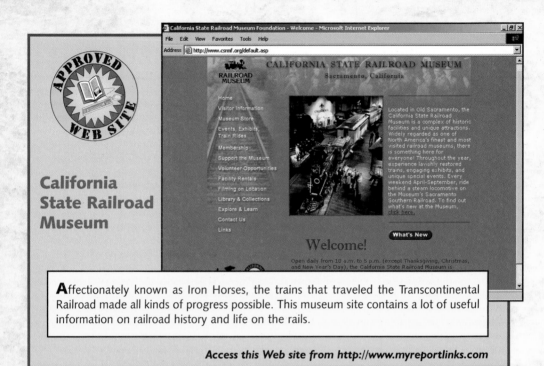

CALIFORNIA STATE RAILROAD MUSEUM
Sacramento, California

California State Railroad Museum

Home
Visitor Information
Museum Store
Events, Exhibits, Train Rides
Membership
Support the Museum
Volunteer Opportunities
Facility Rentals
Filming on Location
Library & Collections
Explore & Learn
Contact Us
Links

Located in Old Sacramento, the California State Railroad Museum is a complex of historic facilities and unique attractions. Widely regarded as one of North America's finest and most visited railroad museums, there is something here for everyone! Throughout the year, experience lavishly restored trains, engaging exhibits, and unique special events. Every weekend April-September, ride behind a steam locomotive on the Museum's Sacramento Southern Railroad. To find out what's new at the Museum, click here.

Welcome!

What's New

Open daily from 10 a.m. to 5 p.m. (except Thanksgiving, Christmas, and New Year's Day), the California State Railroad Museum is

Affectionately known as Iron Horses, the trains that traveled the Transcontinental Railroad made all kinds of progress possible. This museum site contains a lot of useful information on railroad history and life on the rails.

Access this Web site from http://www.myreportlinks.com

route. In New York, Judah was carried off the boat on a stretcher, and he died a few days later.

Meanwhile, in October 1863, the Central Pacific had finally laid its first rails—but Theodore Judah never heard the news. On hearing of Judah's death, Doc Strong resigned from the Central Pacific board. The Big Four were left completely in charge.

Eastern Financial Games

The Pacific Railroad Act called for the appointment of a board of commissioners for the Union Pacific Railroad line. The vice president was Thomas Clark Durant, a doctor of ophthalmology and a successful businessman, who had been involved with smaller railroad projects.

By ignoring some legalities, Durant managed to control $2.2 million worth of shares in the Union Pacific Railroad.[6] He distributed both cash and railroad shares to members of Congress and other influential people. Congress revised the railroad bill to increase government support for the project.

Crédit Mobilier

Under Durant's leadership, the Union Pacific directors bought a small company called Crédit Mobilier and used it to set up a top-secret corporation. In most grand financial ventures, investors had to risk everything they owned. But Crédit Mobilier protected its investors from any such risk. They could only lose the money they had invested.

In a clever shuffle, Crédit Mobilier got the contract to build the railroad and charged the Union Pacific for the work. As a result, building the Union Pacific rail line would become very expensive. Durant and a select group of associates would become very rich.

In 1867, Durant was challenged for control of Crédit Mobilier by investor Oliver Ames and his brother, Congressman Oakes Ames. Congressman Ames freely distributed railroad stock to other members of Congress. He was able to temporarily

Congressman Oakes Ames was a representative from Massachusetts.

kick Durant off of the railroad board, but eventually they all had to share power.

Choosing the Eastern Route

As Ted Judah had done in the Sierra Nevadas, surveyors Grenville Dodge and Peter Dey laid out the route for the eastern railway line. The land was easier going for much of the way, but Colorado's Rocky Mountains had to be taken into consideration. For most of the route, there were no maps. The only way to find out what was over the next hill was to go there and look.

Grenville Dodge loved the outdoors. He had spent a lot of time wandering along the Platte River Valley, and he and his wife had settled there. Dodge was also interested in a transcontinental railroad. When Lincoln was running for president, Dodge went to the Republican convention in Chicago to help get Lincoln nominated.

During the Civil War, Dodge was a general in the Union army. He laid railroad track for the army and repaired sabotaged lines. While Congress was debating the Pacific Railroad Act, Dodge was in a hospital recovering from wounds. Thomas Clark Durant and others approached him to leave the army and work with the Union Pacific. Dodge was firm in his belief that his first duty was to fight for the Union army.

Grenville Dodge was chosen to be in charge of construction on the Union Pacific railway.

Dodge was twenty-eight years old when President Lincoln had to choose a starting point for the Union Pacific tracks. Lincoln talked with Dodge, who described a relatively flat route along the Platte River. So Lincoln decided to start the line in Council Bluffs, Iowa.

▶ Who Would Build It?

By 1863, it was time to start digging. The physical work on the Transcontinental Railroad could begin, but who could actually build such a thing? Where would they find the laborers who would do the work?

Between 1847 and 1854, more than a million and a half Irish had immigrated to the United States to escape famine in their own country. As the Transcontinental Railroad got started, many Chinese began to immigrate to the West Coast for similar reasons. The largest numbers of workers on the Central Pacific would be Chinese; on the Union Pacific, the majority would be Irish.

Chapter 4

BUILDING THE RAILROAD, 1863—1869

Laying train tracks across the entire continent was a gigantic job. Many Americans did not believe it would ever get done. They thought that short sections might be completed, and that even those would be beneficial to certain states and territories. But a transcontinental railroad? To most, it still seemed impossible.

The Central Pacific had started laying track in October 1863. In December 1863, the Union Pacific broke ground with a gala ceremony in Omaha, Nebraska. When the American Civil War was finished, the Union Pacific would actually get started.

▶ A Train Ambush and a Funeral Train

A train ambush helped to end the Civil War. In April 1865, Union troops seized a supply train that was headed for Confederate general Robert E. Lee's camp in Virginia. Without any hope of supplies, Lee surrendered to General Ulysses S. Grant on April 9. The Civil War was over.

Masses of men would soon be released from service, and they would be looking for work.

On April 14, President Abraham Lincoln was assassinated. His body was carried to Illinois by train, in a special Pullman car. Lincoln had gotten the Transcontinental Railroad started; others would have to see the job through.

▶ Building the Central Pacific

The first part of the Central Pacific route was not hard to build. Near Sacramento, the route was fairly flat. Collis P. Huntington moved to New York to raise money and take care of shipments of iron and other materials, while Charles Crocker oversaw the construction.

Work crews on the early part of the line were mostly Irish, directly managed by construction boss James Harvey Strobridge. By 1865, the Central Pacific was well funded by the state and federal governments. The railroad was already earning money, carrying passengers and freight 31 miles between Sacramento and Newcastle.

It soon became clear that the Central Pacific needed a lot more laborers—over four thousand, and they only had about eight hundred. California still had a small population, and many men preferred to work near the gold fields or in towns. Few wanted to take on the Sierra Nevada

Mountains. There was a fear that they would not be able to find enough workers.

▶ Chinese Immigrants

Flood and famine had affected some parts of China for many years. Like those from other nations, Chinese immigrants moved to America to find a better way of life. They crossed the Pacific Ocean crammed into the holds below the decks of sailing ships. To pay their passage, they indentured themselves to Chinese companies in

▲ *A Central Pacific railway camp near the Humboldt River Canyon in Nevada.*

California. That meant they had to work for a period of time—usually five years—to pay off their debt. Afterward, some Chinese immigrants scattered into the gold fields in search of riches. Others found jobs as cooks and laborers in towns and cities.

In California, prejudice against the Chinese was strong. Although they were known to be industrious, few Chinese had been hired for railroad work. Strobridge at first refused to hire them. He did not think they would be strong enough to do the work. But then Crocker talked Strobridge into hiring a few Chinese laborers. Those men worked so well that he hired more. Soon the Central Pacific was actively recruiting Chinese labor—both in California and in China.

▶ Hard Workers

The white railroad workers earned thirty dollars per month, and that included meals. At first the Chinese were paid twenty-six dollars per month and had to take care of their own food. However, their wages were soon raised to thirty dollars.[1] The Chinese were excellent workers and did not hesitate to take on the challenge of laying track in the Sierra Nevada Mountains. They organized themselves into teams. They bought and cooked their own food, which was much better fare than the beans, beef, potatoes, and bread the other

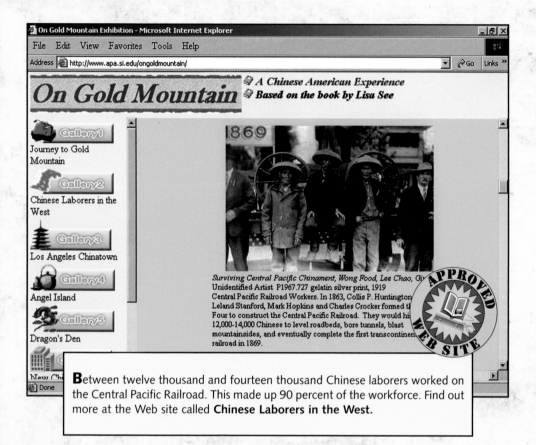

On Gold Mountain Exhibition - Microsoft Internet Explorer

File   Edit   View   Favorites   Tools   Help

Address http://www.apa.si.edu/ongoldmountain/   Go   Links »

On Gold Mountain
A Chinese American Experience
Based on the book by Lisa See

Gallery1
Journey to Gold Mountain

Gallery2
Chinese Laborers in the West

Gallery3
Los Angeles Chinatown

Gallery4
Angel Island

Gallery5
Dragon's Den

New Ch...

Done

1869

Surviving Central Pacific Chinament, Wong Food, Lee Chao, Gy
Unidentified Artist P1967.727 gelatin silver print, 1919
Central Pacific Railroad Workers. In 1863, Collis P. Huntington
Leland Stanford, Mark Hopkins and Charles Crocker formed th
Four to construct the Central Pacific Railroad. They would hi
12,000-14,000 Chinese to level roadbeds, bore tunnels, blast
mountainsides, and eventually complete the first transcontinen
railroad in 1869.

APPROVED WEB SITE

Between twelve thousand and fourteen thousand Chinese laborers worked on the Central Pacific Railroad. This made up 90 percent of the workforce. Find out more at the Web site called **Chinese Laborers in the West.**

workers ate. They bathed and washed their clothes often, to the amazement of the white workers.

▶ Working Across the "Cape"

For the most part, the Central Pacific line followed the same route that Ted Judah had surveyed across the Sierra Nevadas. The men worked their way across the mountains, removing trees, clearing the path of stumps and rocks.

They nicknamed one cliff face "Cape Horn" because it seemed as dangerous as the South

American cape that had to be rounded by ship.[2] It was a steep slope with the American River 2,000 feet below. Judah and the earlier surveyors had seen it and decided it could be used, but even they had not ventured out across that cliff.

Inch by inch, the Chinese work crews moved across the cliff face, cutting a narrow shelf. After a month, they were still creeping along. Then it is thought that someone made a suggestion to try a different way of doing things. In China, some of these men had worked on similar cliffs above the Yangtze River. There, they had been lowered from above in large baskets to do this kind of job.

Chinese-American Contribution to Transcontinental Railroad

The Central Pacific Railroad Photographic History Museum provides a large collection devoted to the Chinese who worked the Central Pacific section of the Transcontinental Railroad. Articles, photographs, and other historical documents are included.

Access this Web site from http://www.myreportlinks.com

As the men requested, Strobridge brought in reeds and rope. The Chinese wove waist-high baskets and rigged them to be lowered over Cape Horn. A worker in a basket would hand drill a hole in the cliff face. He would tamp powder into the hole and manage to light a fuse in spite of the constant wind. Then he would yell and scramble out of his basket up the ropes, as those above hauled him up.[3] That method of dynamiting the cliff sped the work up considerably.

Tunneling Through the Mountain

Tunnels were the other challenge faced by Central Pacific crews. The men had to build at least ten tunnels large enough to allow a locomotive's smokestack to pass through. The longest would be 1,600 feet. Their progress through the granite mountain was 7 inches per day.[4]

In *Nothing Like It in the World,* historian Stephen E. Ambrose describes the work:

> Of all the backbreaking labor that went into the building of the CP and the UP, of all the dangers inherent in the work, this was the worst. . . . The man holding the drill had to be steady or he would get hit by the sledgehammer. The man swinging the hammer had to have muscles like steel. When a hole was at last big enough for the black powder, the crew would fill it, set a fuse, yell as loud as they could while running out of the range of the blast,

and hope. Sometimes the fuse worked, sometimes it didn't.[5]

Rainstorms and snowstorms made the work even more dangerous. Avalanches covered tunnels and killed workers. In one case, sixteen men were buried in a log house. When the storm ended, rescuers digging through the 15 feet to the house met two men digging their way out. The men had been buried for fourteen hours; three had died.[6]

A new explosive would soon make the work easier, if not less dangerous.

Nitro

In April 1866, a crate that had been shipped from Germany to San Francisco exploded when workmen pried it open. The blast leveled the Wells Fargo office and other nearby buildings. Fifteen people were killed and many more were badly injured.

The explosive substance was nitroglycerine, which had been invented two years earlier by an Italian chemist, Ascanio Sobrero. Nitroglycerine was eight times as powerful as the black blasting powder that was then in use. Only a little of the substance would create a violent blast. But nitroglycerine tended to explode without warning, especially if bumped hard in transport.

Crocker and Strobridge were already experimenting with nitroglycerine to help build the

Central Pacific Railroad. Soon after the San Francisco devastation, another explosion on the line north of Sacramento killed six men. The public found it easy to imagine what could happen if there was a blast on a crowded ship or train, and protested feverishly.[7] The transportation of nitroglycerine was banned in California.

Then a chemist from England—James Howden—told Crocker that he could manufacture the substance safely on the work site. Howden proved true to his word, and Crocker put nitroglycerine into use cutting through the Sierra Nevadas. Progress on the tunnels increased from 7 inches to 2 feet per day.[8]

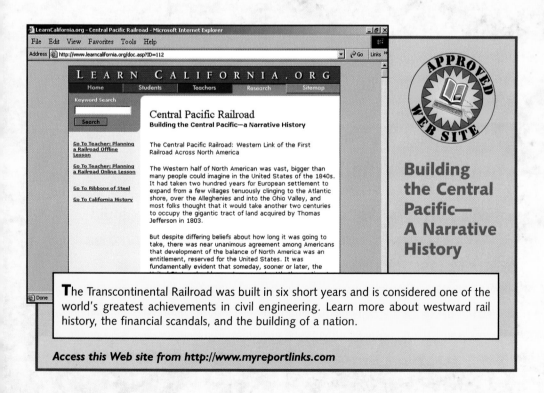

The Transcontinental Railroad was built in six short years and is considered one of the world's greatest achievements in civil engineering. Learn more about westward rail history, the financial scandals, and the building of a nation.

Access this Web site from http://www.myreportlinks.com

No one knows how many lives were lost to nitroglycerine in Central Pacific tunnels. Once they were through the summit, Crocker decided not to use it anymore. But in early 1869, Union Pacific crews also occasionally put nitroglycerine to use in Utah canyons.

Building the Union Pacific

In July 1865 the Union Pacific finally started laying rails, without any fanfare. As Central Pacific crews were painstakingly making their way through the Sierra Nevadas, Union Pacific crews started creeping across the Great Plains. In 1866, Thomas C. Durant hired General Grenville Dodge as chief engineer of the project.

Almost all the workers on the Union Pacific were either soldiers recently released from service or Irish immigrants. They were young, usually long haired, and they wore their revolvers at their sides. Their long brass-buttoned overcoats—some Union blue and some Confederate gray—were left over from their uniforms.[9] They were joined by freed slaves and newly arrived European immigrants. In Utah, Mormon workers also worked on the Union Pacific line.

The workers slept in bunks inside a railroad car, or outside on top of the car when the night was hot. They were paid from $2.50 to $4 a day, and they were charged $5 per week for food and sleeping space.[10] Sometimes the men's pay failed to arrive, and the workers would strike. These men were used to working as a team and fighting as a team when necessary. They made an efficient and independent workforce.

Camps were set up along the construction route with workshops, offices, bunks, and food supplies for thousands of men. These camps were moved forward every day. Union Pacific laborers could be spread out over 20 miles. After the surveyors came teams of other railroad workers with specific jobs. Alongside the railroad teams

American Experience | Transcontinental Railroad | Gallery - Microsoft Internet Explorer

File   Edit   View   Favorites   Tools   Help

Address http://www.pbs.org/wgbh/amex/tcrr/gallery/gal_tcrr_11.html

PBS HOME   PROGRAMS A-Z   TV SCHEDULES   SUPPORT PBS   SHOP PBS   SEARCH PBS

AMERICAN EXPERIENCE

TRANSCONTINENTAL RAILROAD

THE FILM & MORE
SPECIAL FEATURES
TIMELINE
GALLERY
PEOPLE & EVENTS
TEACHER'S GUIDE

Gallery: Transcontinental Railroad   ◀ 11 of 12 ▶

APPROVED WEB SITE

Workers for both the Union Pacific and the Central Pacific railroads usually ate meat, potatoes, bread, and beans. Chinese workers, however, ate vegetables and seafood. Find out more details at the **Transcontinental Railroad Web site.**

EDITOR'S CHOICE

worked telegraph crews, putting up poles and communication lines.

The surveyors chose a specific route. Behind them came the graders, living in tents or sleeping in the open.

The Graders

The bed—or grade—for the train track had to be laid out 2 feet higher than the ground so the track

△ The directors of the Union Pacific Railroad stop to pose for a picture while inspecting the progress of the railroad 250 miles west of Omaha, Nebraska. The group also includes capitalists, newspapermen, and other prominent figures invited by the railroad's directors.

would not be flooded out. The workmen dug, filled wheelbarrows, and took it to the grade to build up the height. After the hard day's work, graders and other workers would play cards, sing songs, and drink.

Stable bosses oversaw the use of horses, mules, and wagons that hauled the supplies and the loads of dirt. The driver assigned to a team was expected to turn it in at the end of the season in good condition. Other bosses watched the men to make sure than no one was loafing.

▶ Tracklayers

Tracklayers followed the graders. As they laid track and railroad ties, flat cars rolled up behind them with rails and other supplies. Gangs of men loaded the supplies on horse-drawn lorries (low rail cars without sides) and took them to the end of the track.

Other work gangs laid the rails in place and drove the spikes that held them down. Then the supply lorries moved a few feet forward, and the process was repeated. It took three mallet strokes to drive in each spike. There were ten spikes in each rail, and four hundred rails were laid in each mile of track.[11]

As Union Pacific workers proceeded, the Great Plains was developing into an area of chaos and brutality.

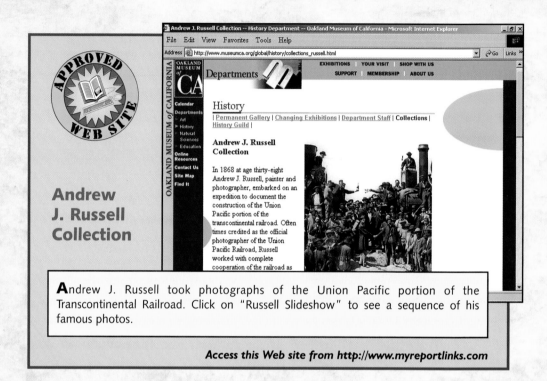

APPROVED WEB SITE

Andrew J. Russell Collection

Andrew J. Russell Collection -- History Department -- Oakland Museum of California - Microsoft Internet Explorer

File   Edit   View   Favorites   Tools   Help

Address http://www.museumca.org/global/history/collections_russell.html   Go   Links

OAKLAND MUSEUM of CALIFORNIA

OAKLAND MUSEUM of CA

Departments

EXHIBITIONS | YOUR VISIT | SHOP WITH US
SUPPORT | MEMBERSHIP | ABOUT US

Calendar
Departments
• Art
▶ History
• Natural
  Sciences
• Education
Online
Resources
Contact Us
Site Map
Find It

History

| Permanent Gallery | Changing Exhibitions | Department Staff | Collections |
History Guild |

Andrew J. Russell Collection

In 1868 at age thirty-eight
Andrew J. Russell, painter and
photographer, embarked on an
expedition to document the
construction of the Union
Pacific portion of the
transcontinental railroad. Often
times credited as the official
photographer of the Union
Pacific Railroad, Russell
worked with complete
cooperation of the railroad as

Andrew J. Russell took photographs of the Union Pacific portion of the Transcontinental Railroad. Click on "Russell Slideshow" to see a sequence of his famous photos.

Access this Web site from http://www.myreportlinks.com

▶ American Indians

Many American Indians had watched wagon trains of settlers cross their land. The buffalo herds essential to their survival were being killed off. Now the American Indians were becoming alarmed at the increase in settlers and military troops on the plains.

In 1864, United States cavalrymen killed 150 unarmed Cheyenne and Arapaho people in a raid known as the Sand Creek Massacre. Many of the victims were women and children. In early 1865, survivors of Sand Creek joined other tribes in some of the most brutal attacks on settlers.

As the railroad progressed across the plains, Dodge ordered his soldiers to "attack and kill every male Indian over twelve years of age."[12] Chief Red Cloud and other American Indian leaders led the Sioux and Cheyenne against the invaders. By the fall of 1865, it became clear that the United States troops were making the situation worse, not better. Then the government began working out treaties with various American Indian peoples.

Even during this time, the Pawnee and some other American Indians remained friendly to the settlers and railroad builders.

Joining the Lines

The backbreaking work went on year after year. In 1868, the Union Pacific began to work its way across Wyoming. The Central Pacific finally made it through the Sierra Nevada. In June 1868, the first passenger train crossed the mountains to Reno, Nevada.[13]

On flatter land, the Central Pacific workers no longer measured their progress in feet per day. Now they could think in terms of miles. Both teams raced across the plains. More and more Americans began to believe that they might actually see a transcontinental railroad in their own lifetime.

Some American Indian peoples began to resent the intrusion on their lifestyle that the construction of the railroad was causing. This engraving shows the artist's interpretation of Cheyenne Indians attacking a working party on the Union Pacific Railroad.

Since no location had been set for the lines to be joined, the surveyors and graders for each side kept to their own intended routes. Those crews actually passed each other, working in opposite directions on parallel lines.[14]

The Meeting

In April 1869, after months of lobbying and argument, Promontory Summit, Utah, was chosen as the meeting place for the two lines. Both rail lines were within about fifty miles away from that point. The surveyors and graders who had passed the meeting point stopped work and turned back.

Now the two railroad companies raced each other to Promontory Summit, each trying to lay more track per day than the other. Sometimes teams from one group intimidated workers of the other in an effort to slow their progress. The Union Pacific crew laid 4 miles of track in one day. The Central Pacific laid 6 miles. Then Union Pacific laid 7 miles in a day. In an amazing final push, the Central Pacific workers laid a record-breaking 10 miles in one day.

▷ Last-Minute Concerns

Thomas Durant and other Union Pacific officials rode westward on a train headed to the Summit. They were approaching the Utah state line when suddenly they were surrounded by angry railroad workers. A pile of railroad ties on the track forced their train to a halt. Rifle shots rang out. Members of a mob uncoupled Durant's car from the engine, moved the railroad ties, and waved the locomotive to continue on without its cars.

These men had not been paid for months, and now they wanted their money—over $200,000 in all. There are conflicting reports as to what happened next. Telegrams flew back and forth, some threatening. Troops were called out but not used. Finally, the money was raised, the men were paid, and Durant was allowed to continue on to the ceremony.[15]

A Central Pacific passenger train came from the West, followed by Leland Stanford's own

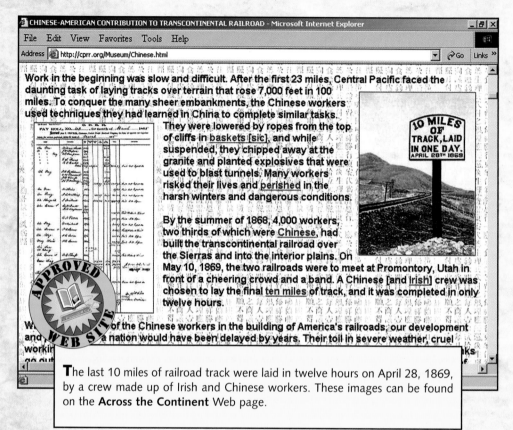

CHINESE-AMERICAN CONTRIBUTION TO TRANSCONTINENTAL RAILROAD - Microsoft Internet Explorer

File   Edit   View   Favorites   Tools   Help

Address http://cprr.org/Museum/Chinese.html   Go   Links

Work in the beginning was slow and difficult. After the first 23 miles, Central Pacific faced the daunting task of laying tracks over terrain that rose 7,000 feet in 100 miles. To conquer the many sheer embankments, the Chinese workers used techniques they had learned in China to complete similar tasks. They were lowered by ropes from the top of cliffs in baskets [sic], and while suspended, they chipped away at the granite and planted explosives that were used to blast tunnels. Many workers risked their lives and perished in the harsh winters and dangerous conditions.

By the summer of 1868, 4,000 workers, two thirds of which were Chinese, had built the transcontinental railroad over the Sierras and into the interior plains. On May 10, 1869, the two railroads were to meet at Promontory, Utah in front of a cheering crowd and a band. A Chinese [and Irish] crew was chosen to lay the final ten miles of track, and it was completed in only twelve hours.

W... ...of the Chinese workers in the building of America's railroads, our development and ... a nation would have been delayed by years. Their toil in severe weather, cruel workin...

The last 10 miles of railroad track were laid in twelve hours on April 28, 1869, by a crew made up of Irish and Chinese workers. These images can be found on the **Across the Continent** Web page.

special train. The Californians brought with them a special spike made of gold—to be used to join the lines. They also brought a highly polished railroad tie made of laurel wood, and a hammer with a silver head.[16]

The train from the West arrived at Promontory on May 7. The tracks were supposed to be joined on May 8, but the Union Pacific train had been held up by the angry laborers and again by a washed-out track. The people of Sacramento,

California, held parades and celebrations on May 8 regardless.

On May 10, with trains from both the West and East finally present, the two lines were ready to be officially joined. After all the digging and blasting; after all the tunnels, bridges, and miles of track; after all the hard work, injuries, and deaths; the Transcontinental Railroad was about to be completed.

Chapter 5

SUPPORTERS, BUILDERS, AND PROFITEERS

Many thousands of people were involved in building the Transcontinental Railroad. The names of most workers will never be known. Bodies that were buried along the way or shipped back to China remain unidentified. Some of those who completed the job went on to work on other railroads or in other trades. Some settled down close to the line, in one of the new towns or on nearby farmlands.

Of those whose names are recorded, only a handful can be covered in this book. Longer reference books and Web sites include more about those who struggled to get the project started, to build the lines, and to profit from the work. The following brief biographies are about some of the best-known characters who were involved with the Transcontinental Railroad.

▷ Charles Crocker

Charles Crocker (1822–88) quit school and went to work at age twelve. He owned a newspaper distribution agency in New York until his family

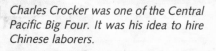

Charles Crocker was one of the Central Pacific Big Four. It was his idea to hire Chinese laborers.

moved to Indiana. There, Crocker worked on the family farm until he left home at age seventeen. He worked at a sawmill, and ran an iron mine and foundry.[1] In 1849, Crocker traveled overland by wagon to the gold fields, tried prospecting, and then became a merchant. In 1860, he became one of the Big Four partners in the Central Pacific. His own Charles Crocker & Company was put in charge of building the railroad. Crocker was responsible for hiring the Chinese laborers who did the job, and he was the only one of the Big Four who actually spent time working on the line.

▶ Jefferson Davis

Jefferson Davis (1808–89) attended school in Mississippi and went on to graduate from West Point in 1828. In 1835, he resigned from the military to marry and run a cotton plantation in Mississippi. He was elected to the House of Representatives, returned to the military to lead a regiment in the Mexican-American War, and was then elected to the U.S. Senate. Davis served as secretary of war in the Cabinet of President Franklin Pierce, during which time he advised that a transcontinental railroad be built, beginning in the South. Davis again served in the Senate until he resigned in 1861, when the state of Mississippi seceded from the Union. Davis was elected president of the Confederacy in 1861. After the war, he was captured and imprisoned until 1867 while he was charged with treason. He never stood trial.

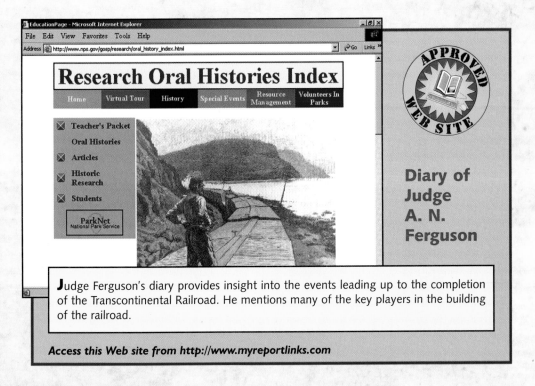

Diary of Judge A. N. Ferguson

Judge Ferguson's diary provides insight into the events leading up to the completion of the Transcontinental Railroad. He mentions many of the key players in the building of the railroad.

Access this Web site from http://www.myreportlinks.com

Grenville M. Dodge

Grenville M. Dodge (1831–1916) was born into a poor family, and began working on railroads at age fourteen, laying track.[2] During the Civil War he became a brigadier general in the Union army. Dodge organized a spy system for General Grant and intercepted Confederate raiding parties. He built military railroads and destroyed enemy tracks. In 1865, while leading the U.S. Army's campaign against the Plains Indians, Dodge discovered a pass through the Black Hills that the Union Pacific would use. In 1866, Dodge resigned from the army and became the Union Pacific's chief engineer. He and Thomas C. Durant had many bitter disputes. When the Crédit Mobilier scandal was under investigation, federal agents could not locate Dodge, who had apparently disappeared into the wilderness. He and his wife later made their home in Council Bluffs, Iowa, the Union Pacific starting point that Lincoln had chosen on Dodge's advice.

Thomas Clark Durant

Thomas Clark Durant (1820–85) was born into a well-to-do family in Massachusetts. He graduated from medical school and although he left medicine for a career in business, Durant always used the title of "doctor." He built sections of railroads in several states and founded the Missouri

Thomas Clark Durant was instrumental in the creation of the Union Pacific Railroad. He founded Crédit Mobilier, but was not implicated in the scandal the company was involved in.

& Mississippi Railroad. During the Civil War, he made money smuggling cotton illegally from the Confederate states. Durant gained control of the Union Pacific railroad and used the Crédit Mobilier to become even wealthier. Although he escaped charges in the scandal that followed, Durant spent much of the rest of his life struggling with legal complications from his Union Pacific deals.[3]

Ulysses S. Grant

Ulysses S. Grant (1822–85) was the eighteenth president of the United States (1869–77). As a child, Grant was small, sensitive, quiet, and often teased by other kids.[4] As a Civil War general, Grant led the Union forces. He accepted the surrender of Confederate general Robert E. Lee at Appomattox Court House in 1865. Grant was elected president while the Transcontinental Railroad was being completed, and he was one of its strongest supporters.

Mark Hopkins

Mark Hopkins (1813–78) was born in Henderson, New York. When gold was discovered in California, he hurried west. But Hopkins soon gave up prospecting and started a grocery store in Sacramento—right next to the hardware store owned by Collis P. Huntington. Hopkins became one of the Big Four partners in the Central Pacific Railroad. He was a quiet man who kept the books and records, and he tried to keep the other partners from getting involved in even riskier projects. In 1872, when the Union Pacific partners were under congressional investigation, it was believed to be Hopkins who burned the Central Pacific books.[5] This was never proven. Even after he became wealthy,

Mark Hopkins was a financier and promoter of the Central Pacific Railroad. One of the Big Four, he escaped blame in the scandals that followed the railroad's completion.

Hopkins lived a very simple life with his family in San Francisco.

▶ Collis P. Huntington

Collis P. Huntington (1821–1900) was born in Connecticut. As a boy, he worked on a farm, saved his money, and at age fifteen started selling clocks in several states.[6] Huntington set out for California during the Gold Rush, taking the Panama route. When his journey was held up for several months, Huntington made a profit trading goods in Panama. He opened a hardware store in Sacramento, and soon he and Mark Hopkins became partners. Huntington was one of the Big Four investors in the Central Pacific Railroad Company. He later built railroads in other areas and invested in a Virginia shipyard. He became a patron of the arts and a contributor to funding for the education of African Americans and American Indians.

Collis P. Huntington was another ▶ one of the Big Four backers of the Central Pacific railroad.

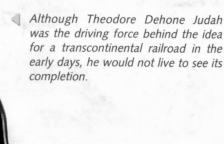

Although Theodore Dehone Judah was the driving force behind the idea for a transcontinental railroad in the early days, he would not live to see its completion.

▶ Theodore Judah

Theodore Judah (1826–63) lived in Troy, New York, as a boy. His father, an Episcopal minister, died when Judah was young. Ted Judah studied engineering as a young man, and by age eighteen, he was a trained railroad surveyor—ready to enter a brand-new field. After he married at twenty-one, he and his wife, Anna, moved around from one railroad job to another. Judah also worked on the construction of the Erie Canal. His enthusiasm for railroads and his dreams for a cross-country project earned him the nickname "Crazy Judah." In 1861, he and his survey team laid out the route through the Sierra Nevada Mountains. Although Judah's surveys gained financial support for the railroad, he was cut out of the Central Pacific partnership. On his way east to find new financial backing, Judah became ill crossing the Isthmus of Panama and died soon after he reached New York City.

▷ Abraham Lincoln

Abraham Lincoln (1809–65) was the sixteenth president of the United States (1861–65). He was born in a log cabin in Kentucky. When he was eight, his family moved to Indiana, which Lincoln described as a "wild region, with many bears and other wild animals still in the woods."[7] His mother died when he was nine. As a young man, Lincoln worked at hard manual labor and had little formal education, but he taught himself to read, write, and do arithmetic. Over the following years, Lincoln worked on riverboats and at odd jobs, was in the military, became a member of the Illinois legislature, earned a law license, and served a term in the United States Congress. He returned to his law practice, but then challenged Stephen Douglas over the Kansas-Nebraska Act of 1854. Lincoln's backers propelled him to the presidency in 1860. He supported western settlement and the Transcontinental Railroad, even while the nation fought a Civil War. In 1865, Lincoln was assassinated during his second presidential term.

▷ James K. Polk

James K. Polk (1795–1849) was the eleventh president of the United States (1845–49). He was a studious, industrious learner, who graduated with honors from college. Polk became a lawyer and then entered politics. He served in the Tennessee State legislature, in the House of Representatives, and as governor of Tennessee. He ran for president on a platform that emphasized expanding United States territory. As president, Polk negotiated with Great Britain the current boundary between Canada and the northwestern United States. His pressure on Mexico to sell California resulted in the Mexican-American War. After the American forces won the war, Mexico agreed to transfer New Mexico and California to the United States for $15 million. This included much of what is now considered to be the southwestern United States.

George Pullman

George Pullman (1831–97) invented the Pullman sleeping car. Although he dropped out of school at age fourteen, Pullman worked hard as a merchant, cabinetmaker, and building contractor. He had an idea for a luxury passenger railroad car, and remodeled some old train cars into comfortable sleeping cars. After President Abraham Lincoln was assassinated, the president's body was transported to Illinois in a specially built Pullman car. In 1867, Thomas C. Durant took an interest in Pullman's cars and used them on the Union

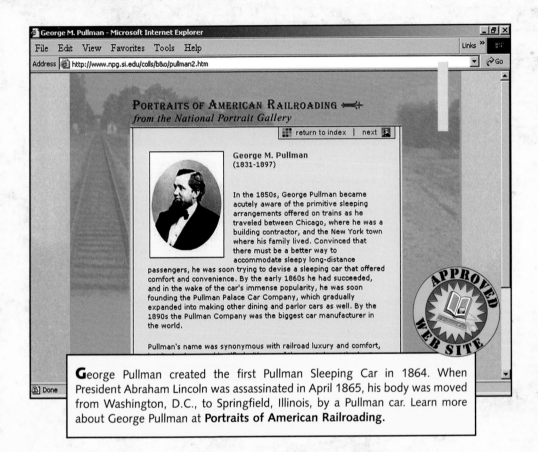

PORTRAITS OF AMERICAN RAILROADING
from the National Portrait Gallery

return to index | next

George M. Pullman
(1831-1897)

In the 1850s, George Pullman became acutely aware of the primitive sleeping arrangements offered on trains as he traveled between Chicago, where he was a building contractor, and the New York town where his family lived. Convinced that there must be a better way to accommodate sleepy long-distance passengers, he was soon trying to devise a sleeping car that offered comfort and convenience. By the early 1860s he had succeeded, and in the wake of the car's immense popularity, he was soon founding the Pullman Palace Car Company, which gradually expanded into making other dining and parlor cars as well. By the 1890s the Pullman Company was the biggest car manufacturer in the world.

Pullman's name was synonymous with railroad luxury and comfort,

George Pullman created the first Pullman Sleeping Car in 1864. When President Abraham Lincoln was assassinated in April 1865, his body was moved from Washington, D.C., to Springfield, Illinois, by a Pullman car. Learn more about George Pullman at **Portraits of American Railroading.**

Pacific. Pullman cars added a touch of luxury to train travel, and the Pullman Palace Car Company would also build diners, parlor cars, and observation cars.[8]

Leland Stanford

Leland Stanford (1824–93) was the fifth of eight children. After years of hard work and schooling, he practiced law in New York and Wisconsin. Then, in 1852, he traveled west via the Isthmus of Panama and became a California merchant near the gold fields. Stanford was elected California

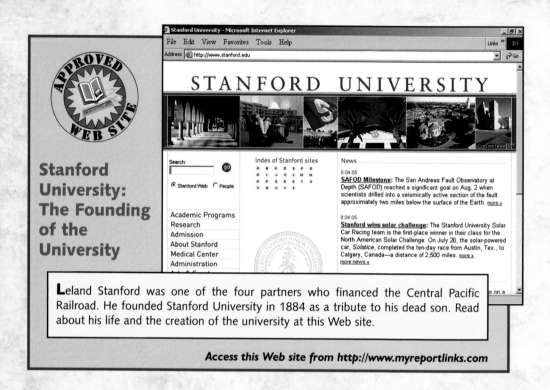

STANFORD UNIVERSITY

Address: http://www.stanford.edu

Search: [ ] go
○ Stanford Web ○ People

Index of Stanford sites
A B C D E F G
H I J K L M N
O P Q R S T U
V W X Y Z

Academic Programs
Research
Admission
About Stanford
Medical Center
Administration

News
8.04.05
SAFOD Milestone: The San Andreas Fault Observatory at Depth (SAFOD) reached a significant goal on Aug. 2 when scientists drilled into a seismically active section of the fault approximately two miles below the surface of the Earth. more »

8.04.05
Stanford wins solar challenge: The Stanford University Solar Car Racing team is the first-place winner in their class for the North American Solar Challenge. On July 26, the solar-powered car, *Solstice*, completed the ten-day race from Austin, Tex., to Calgary, Canada—a distance of 2,500 miles. more »
more news »

Stanford University: The Founding of the University

Leland Stanford was one of the four partners who financed the Central Pacific Railroad. He founded Stanford University in 1884 as a tribute to his dead son. Read about his life and the creation of the university at this Web site.

Access this Web site from http://www.myreportlinks.com

governor in 1861. In 1863 he broke ground at the ceremony that began construction on the Central Pacific Railroad. Governor Stanford was one of the Big Four who invested in the Central Pacific and became wealthy building the railroad. At Promontory Summit, he tapped a gold spike into the final rail. In 1891 he founded Leland Stanford University in honor of his son, who had died of typhoid fever.

Chapter 6

TYING THE EASTERN TO THE WESTERN SEA

On May 10, 1869, the train from the East and one from the West faced each other across a one-rail gap in the Transcontinental Railroad line. Several ceremonial spikes were brought to Promontory Summit for connecting the Union Pacific and Central Pacific lines. One was pure gold. On it were the words "the last spike," the names of Central Pacific dignitaries, and the expected connection date of May 8, 1869. That spike was given to the Stanford Museum in 1892, and that is where it remains. Two other spikes, one silver and one of iron, silver, and gold were similarly inscribed. Not one of these spikes was strong enough to be driven into the ties, so they were tapped into pre-drilled holes by Leland Stanford and Thomas Durant.

The actual last spike was made of polished steel—far more practical than gold or silver. Telegraph wires were wrapped around that spike. When the silver sledgehammer (which was

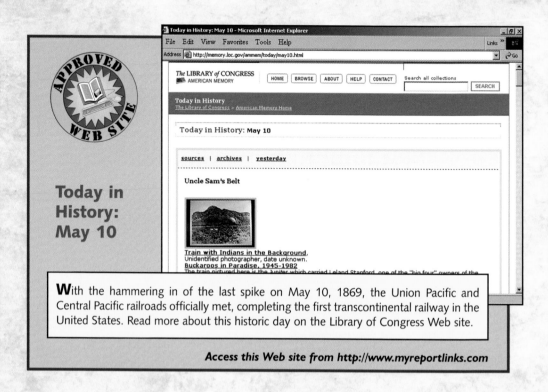

Today in
History:
May 10

Today in History: May 10 - Microsoft Internet Explorer

File   Edit   View   Favorites   Tools   Help   Links »

Address http://memory.loc.gov/ammem/today/may10.html   Go

The LIBRARY of CONGRESS
AMERICAN MEMORY   HOME   BROWSE   ABOUT   HELP   CONTACT   Search all collections   SEARCH

Today in History
The Library of Congress > American Memory Home

Today in History: **May 10**

sources | archives | **yesterday**

Uncle Sam's Belt

Train with Indians in the Background,
Unidentified photographer, date unknown.
Buckaroos in Paradise, 1945-1982
The train pictured here is the *Jupiter* which carried Leland Stanford, one of the "big four" owners of the

With the hammering in of the last spike on May 10, 1869, the Union Pacific and
Central Pacific railroads officially met, completing the first transcontinental railway in the
United States. Read more about this historic day on the Library of Congress Web site.

Access this Web site from http://www.myreportlinks.com

also wired) struck the spike, people across the
country could hear the blow. In San Francisco
and New York, cannon had been placed facing
toward the ocean. Telegraph wires were connected to the cannon, and when the sound of the
hammer blow came through the wire the cannon
all fired.

After the last rail was in place, the Central
Pacific and Union Pacific locomotives moved
slowly forward until their noses touched.
American author and poet Bret Harte imagined
that each engine might brag a bit about its
accomplishments.

"What the Engines Said
Opening of the Pacific Railroad" by Bret Harte

What was it the Engines said,
Pilots touching,—head to head
Facing on the single track,
Half a world behind each back?
This is what the Engines said,
Unreported and unread.

With a prefatory screech,
In a florid Western speech,
Said the engine from the West,
"I am from Sierra's crest;
And, if altitude 's a test,
Why, I reckon, it 's confessed,
That I've done my level best."

▲ This is an image of the joining of the tracks for the Transcontinental Railroad.
The ceremony took place at Promontory Summit in what was then the Utah
Territory.

Said the Engine from the East,

"They who work best talk the least.

S'pose you whistle down your brakes;

What you 've done is no great shakes,—

Pretty fair,—but let our meeting

Be a different kind of greeting.

Let these folks with champagne stuffing,

Not their Engines, do the *puffing*.

"Listen! Where Atlantic beats

Shores of snow and summer heats;

Where the Indian autumn skies

Paint the woods with wampum dies,—

I have chased the flying sun,

Seeing all he looked upon,

Blessing all that he has blest,

Nursing in my iron breast

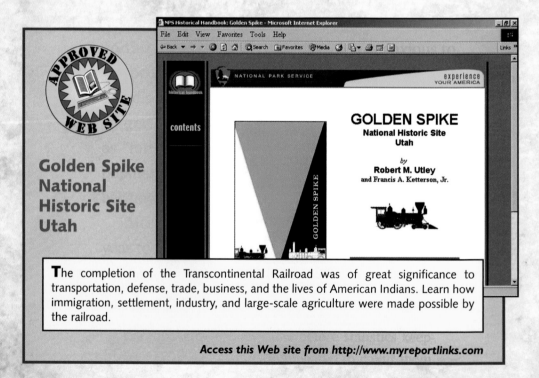

Golden Spike
National
Historic Site
Utah

The completion of the Transcontinental Railroad was of great significance to transportation, defense, trade, business, and the lives of American Indians. Learn how immigration, settlement, industry, and large-scale agriculture were made possible by the railroad.

Access this Web site from http://www.myreportlinks.com

All his vivifying heat,

All his clouds about my crest;

And before my flying feet

Every shadow must retreat."

Said the Western Engine, "Phew!"

And a long, low whistle blew.

"Come, now, really that 's the oddest

Talk for one so very modest.

You brag of your East. *You* do?

Why, *I* bring the East to *you*!

All the Orient, all Cathay,

Find through me the shortest way;

And the sun you follow here

Rises in my hemisphere.

Really,—if one must be rude,—

Length, my friend, ain't longitude."

Said the Union: "Don't reflect, or

I'll run over some Director."

Said the Central: "I 'm Pacific;

But, when riled, I 'm quite terrific.

Yet to-day we shall not quarrel,

Just to show these folks this moral,

How two Engines—in their vision—

Once have met without collision."

That is what the Engines said,

Unreported and unread;

Spoken slightly through the nose,

With a whistle at the close.

Shortcuts Come to Light

The whole way, both the Union Pacific and Central Pacific had built as fast as they could. Both had been intent on speed rather than the quality of their construction. After all, Congress was paying them according to the number of miles of track they laid—$16,000 per mile for flat land, $32,000 dollars for foothills, and $48,000 for track laid in the mountains.[1]

After laying the track for the Transcontinental Railroad was finished, corrections costing hundreds

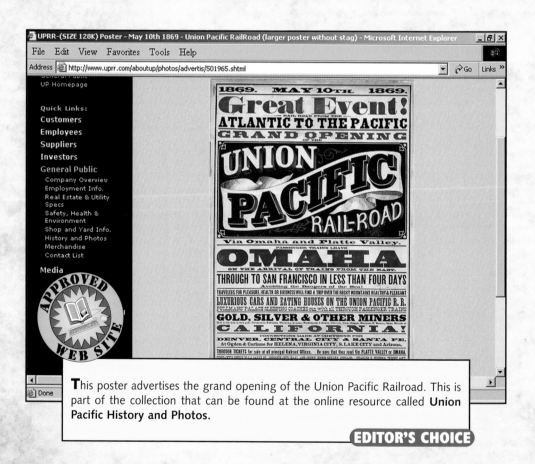

This poster advertises the grand opening of the Union Pacific Railroad. This is part of the collection that can be found at the online resource called **Union Pacific History and Photos**.

EDITOR'S CHOICE

of thousands of dollars had to be made. Tracks that had only recently been laid had to be repaired. New bridges had to be built. But even those necessary repairs did not delay the regular passenger service from beginning on May 15.[2]

Soon, politicians would take a closer look at greater financial losses—the money raked off by the executives of both companies.

▶ Financial Investigations and Scandals

Even while the Union Pacific line was being built, rumors had started about Thomas Durant's personal profits. As the congressional elections of 1872 approached, those suspicions began to get more attention.

In September 1872, the *New York Sun* newspaper ran a story headlined "The King of Frauds." The story described the bribing of congressmen by the Crédit Mobilier. The financial tricks Durant had started playing finally came to light—and became the biggest scandal of the nineteenth century.[3]

The men who held stock in Crédit Mobilier had become very rich, even though the Union Pacific had wound up broke. The stockholders' wealth had come from collecting public funds, paying the lowest possible wages to the workers, and leaving many railroad bills unpaid. The public was furious when the scheme was uncovered.

New Yorker financial columnist James Surowiecki has compared those financial manipulations to scandals of our own century: "The schemes at Enron were far more complex than those at the Crédit Mobilier, but the idea was the same: funnel money from the company to outside businesses controlled by company executives."[4]

Congressional hearings went on for six months. Congressman Oakes Ames—who had distributed a lot of Crédit Mobilier stock to members of Congress—got most of the blame. Durant and a host of others got off completely.

Of course, it is almost certain that the Big Four who controlled the Central Pacific had also been taking as much money as they could get for

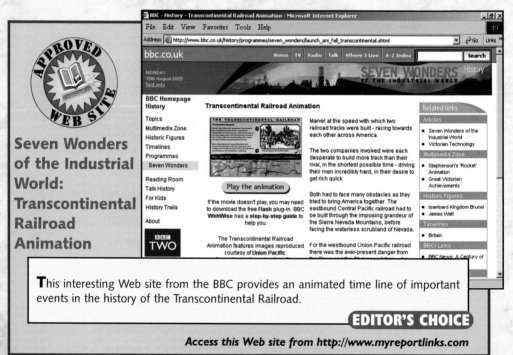

Seven Wonders of the Industrial World: Transcontinental Railroad Animation

This interesting Web site from the BBC provides an animated time line of important events in the history of the Transcontinental Railroad.

EDITOR'S CHOICE

Access this Web site from http://www.myreportlinks.com

themselves. But it turned out that the Central Pacific records had been tossed out and burned. No one could prove that it was not an accident.

Changing Towns

As the railroad extended across the country, towns flourished near the rail line. Other communities that were widely bypassed simply disappeared.

As Union Pacific teams worked along the Platte Valley, rowdy new towns sprang up. When work stopped for the winter, towns appeared at the end of the line almost overnight. Gambling houses, saloons, and dance halls were slapped together from wood and canvas. After all, these railroad men had money to spend and time on their hands. Miners, traders, and some adventurers from the East were also drawn to these wild, lawless places. Gamblers and scoundrels came looking for a quick buck. A Massachusetts newspaper editor got a look at one such town and called it "Hell on Wheels."[5] The name stuck.

When the railroad workers moved on, some "Hell on Wheels" towns disappeared. Other whole towns would take down their shacks, pack up their goods, and follow along the tracks. And some towns remained where they were—though drained of much population.

The railroads had been granted land by the government, and some of it could be sold profitably

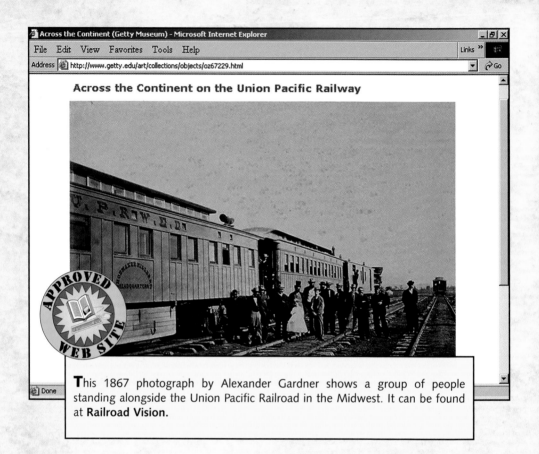

Across the Continent on the Union Pacific Railway

This 1867 photograph by Alexander Gardner shows a group of people standing alongside the Union Pacific Railroad in the Midwest. It can be found at **Railroad Vision.**

as building lots. The railroads wanted new settlers to fill up both their trains and their land. Railroad companies advertised in Europe, encouraging immigration to America.

Railroad companies also advertised cheap rates on immigrant passenger cars. Those low-fare travelers sat on simple benches, and on some lines they could rent straw-filled mattresses from the conductor.[6] Railroads even had box car rates for moving household goods, farm equipment, hired hands, and animals.

Of course, long trains made it easier for large numbers of settlers to move westward. These new people came looking for land and decent places to make a living and raise a family. They moved into some former Hell on Wheels towns and set about cleaning them up. Townspeople and railroad workers together tamed many frontier towns, often using a good bit of necessary force.

Unfortunately, the completion of the Transcontinental Railroad did not open up opportunities for everyone.

▲ *This is a Sierra Nevada ghost town in California. Many towns would boom and bust as a result of the creation of the Transcontinental Railroad.*

Those Who Suffered

The railroad brought settlers, troops, and buffalo hunters into lands that had been occupied by American Indians. The government began to abandon their earlier treaties with American Indians, and new treaties would soon push those people onto reservations. The newcomers hunted buffalo for sport and slaughtered them for their hides. As people of European descent moved westward, traditional American Indian lifestyles were destroyed.

The Chinese had worked hard for years on the Central Pacific line. But after the Transcontinental Railroad was finished, prejudice overcame the pride the nation had taken in their accomplishments. In 1882, Congress passed the Chinese Exclusion Act, suspending immigration. Chinese in America were segregated into "Chinatowns" in major cities and to separate rural areas. They were denied citizenship. They still managed to find work and even start new businesses, including shops, restaurants, and laundries.

Commerce and Communications

In the early 1800s, travel across land was just as it had been for thousands of years—on foot, on horse- or mule-back, and in animal-drawn vehicles. Freight and mail were shipped the same

▲ *This is an artist's drawing of what happened between Chinese and white rail workers at what came to be known as the Rock Springs massacre. Twenty-eight Chinese were killed, 15 were wounded, and 79 of their homes were set afire.*

ways. The Transcontinental Railroad brought dramatic change.

The day before the rail lines were joined, a Wells Fargo Overland Stage arrived at Promontory Summit. A reporter for the *Alta California* newspaper reported, "The four old nags were worn and jaded and the coach showed evidence of long service. The mail matter was delivered to the Central

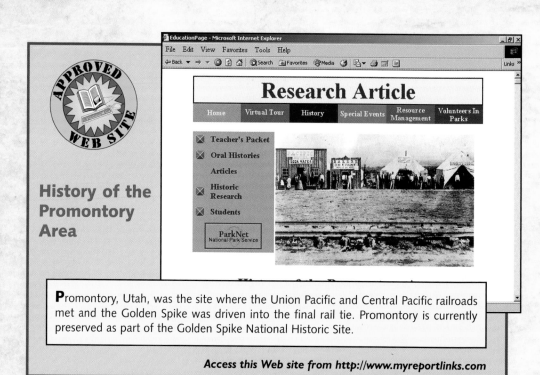

Research Article

| Home | Virtual Tour | History | Special Events | Resource Management | Volunteers In Parks |

Teacher's Packet

Oral Histories

Articles

Historic Research

Students

ParkNet
National Park Service

History of the
Promontory
Area

Promontory, Utah, was the site where the Union Pacific and Central Pacific railroads met and the Golden Spike was driven into the final rail tie. Promontory is currently preserved as part of the Golden Spike National Historic Site.

Access this Web site from http://www.myreportlinks.com

Pacific Co., and with that dusty, dilapidated coach and team, the old order of things passed away forever."[7]

The overland trip from New York to San Francisco dropped from half a year to seven days. The trip that had cost as much as $1,000 by dangerous water routes now ranged from $65 to $150 by train. (The higher rates included a Pullman sleeping car.) Now goods could be shipped coast to coast quickly and cheaply.

Trade between Europe and Asia via America was not to be what some had expected. In 1869 the Suez Canal opened in Egypt, providing an easier passage from Europe to Asia. But the increase in commerce within the United States was much greater than most had imagined. Before ten years had passed, the railroad was shipping $50 million worth of goods across the country every year.[8]

Railroad lines soon spread northward and southward from the Transcontinental Railroad. By 1900, new lines parallel to the Transcontinental Railroad also ran east and west. More and more of the country was becoming connected by railway transportation and telegraph communication.

▲ This is a replica of Union Pacific train No. 119 that arrived at Promontory, Utah, for the Golden Spike ceremony.

Before the end of the 1800s, buyers could shop from Sears and Montgomery Ward catalogs and get their orders delivered by mail. Department stores opened in major cities, offering products from all over the nation and even from other countries.

Thinking on a National Scale

Other things changed along with speed and prices. For example, each area of the country had previously decided what time of the day it was. But railroads had to publish schedules, so timekeeping had to become more consistent. The country was divided into four time zones, and time took on a new importance in the minds of Americans. New expressions turned up in everyday conversation— "time was," "time is wasting," "time's up," and "the train is leaving the station."[9]

Newly published books and magazines could now be read all over the country while the ideas in them were still fresh. America was on its way to becoming a single transcontinental culture. National politics drew attention from localities that had paid little attention before.

Immigrants from many nations eventually overcame prejudices and brought an international flavor to America. Think how many different kinds of meals a person can eat in our cities and towns today. Chinese restaurants are, of course, among the most popular.

Besides such practical matters, the Transcontinental Railroad and other lines also were a source of stories and songs.

Songs and Legends

Railroad workers sang about their lives and work. For example, Irishmen told how "Paddy Works on the Railway."

▲ *Central Pacific train No. 60 was the other train that arrived at Promontory. This train was nicknamed Jupiter.*

In eighteen hundred forty five,
I found meself more dead than alive
I found meself more dead than alive,
while workin' on the railway.

The Irish also sang to their coworkers, as in "John Chinaman, My Jo."[10]

John Chinaman, my jo, John,
Though folks may at you rail,
Here's blessings on your head, John
And more power to your tail.
But a piece of good advice, John
I'll give you, ere I go
Don't abuse the freedom you enjoy
John Chinaman, my jo.

Some popular railroad songs are thought to be based on the life of a real man, a freed slave. John Henry was a steel driver, a man who swung the hammer to drive a steel shaft into rock. He was making holes for explosives—the same way that the Chinese did when they cut through the Sierra Nevada Mountains. John Henry was such a powerful man that many legends (stories based on actual people) were told about him.

According to most of those legends, a new steam drill was brought in to make the holes in rocks. That threatened the men's jobs, so John Henry challenged the machine to a contest. John Henry beat the machine, but he died from the effort. His story is often told in work songs and folk songs.[11]

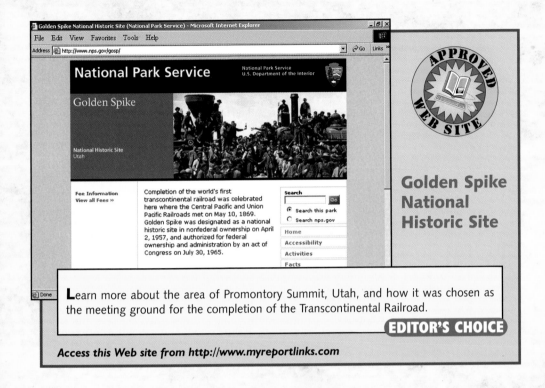

Learn more about the area of Promontory Summit, Utah, and how it was chosen as the meeting ground for the completion of the Transcontinental Railroad.

Access this Web site from http://www.myreportlinks.com

> *John Henry was a steel drivin' man,*
> *He died with a hammah in his han',*
> *Oh, come along boys and line the track*
> *For John Henry ain't never comin' back,*
> *For John Henry ain't never comin' back.*

▶ An American Vision Completed

Traveling across the United States by rail was exciting, and a bargain compared with expensive trips to Europe. Many People reported what they saw in the West. America's incredible building achievement—the Transcontinental Railroad—was bound to stir creative minds. In his poem "Passage to India," Walt Whitman describes a

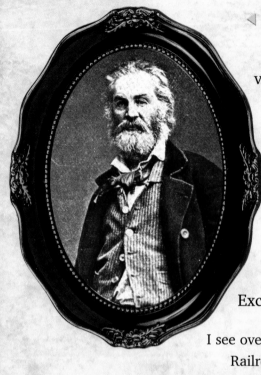
Image of Walt Whitman.

vision of the train crossing over the entire country, connecting the nation together. Because of the Transcontinental Railroad, other Americans also felt the pride and excitement that Whitman expressed:

Excerpt from "Passage to India"

I see over my own continent the Pacific
  Railroad, surmounting every barrier;

I see continual trains of cars winding along the Platte,
  carrying freight and passengers;

I hear the locomotives rushing and roaring, and the shrill
  steam-whistle,

I hear the echoes reverberate through the grandest scenery
  in the world;

I cross the Laramie plains—I note the rocks in grotesque
  shapes—the buttes;

I see the plentiful larkspur and wild onions—the barren,
  colorless, sage-deserts;

I see in glimpses afar, or towering immediately above me,
  the great mountains—I see the Wind River and the
  Wahsatch mountains;

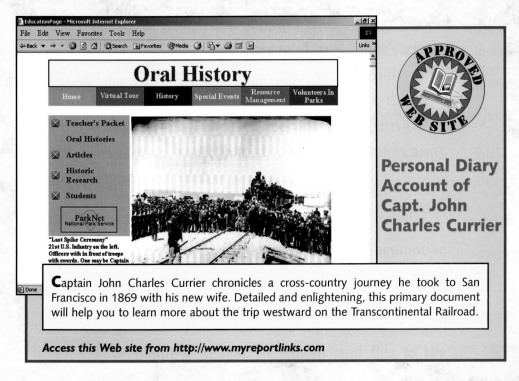

Oral History

Home | Virtual Tour | History | Special Events | Resource Management | Volunteers In Parks

Teacher's Packet

Oral Histories

Articles

Historic Research

Students

ParkNet
National Park Service

"Last Spike Ceremony"
21st U.S. Infantry on the left.
Officers with in front of troops
with swords. One may be Captain

Personal Diary Account of Capt. John Charles Currier

Captain John Charles Currier chronicles a cross-country journey he took to San Francisco in 1869 with his new wife. Detailed and enlightening, this primary document will help you to learn more about the trip westward on the Transcontinental Railroad.

Access this Web site from http://www.myreportlinks.com

I see the Monument mountain and the Eagle's Nest—I pass
 the Promontory—I ascend the Nevadas;

I scan the noble Elk mountain, and wind around its base;

I see the Humboldt range—I thread the valley and cross
 the river,

I see the clear waters of Lake Tahoe—I see forests of
 majestic pines,

Or, crossing the great desert, the alkaline plains,
 I behold enchanting mirages of waters and meadows;

Marking through these, and after all, in duplicate
 slender lines,

Bridging the three or four thousand miles of land travel,
 Tying the Eastern to the Western sea, . . .

Report Links

The Internet sites described below can be accessed at http://www.myreportlinks.com

▶ **Transcontinental Railroad**
Editor's Choice Learn more about the construction of the first transcontinental railroad.

▶ **Golden Spike National Historic Site**
Editor's Choice The National Park Service's Web site for Golden Spike National Historic Park.

▶ **Congress and the American West: The Transcontinental Railroad**
Editor's Choice Primary source documents related to the completion of the railroad.

▶ **Theodore Dehone Judah: Transcontinental Railroad**
Editor's Choice Read about the man who believed a transcontinental railroad could be built.

▶ **Seven Wonders of the Industrial World: Transcontinental Railroad Animation**
Editor's Choice Click on "Play the Animation" for a fun look at the railroad.

▶ **Union Pacific History and Photos**
Editor's Choice The UP Railroad Web site details the history of the Transcontinental Railroad.

▶ **Abraham Lincoln (1861–1865)**
Abraham Lincoln was a supporter of the railroad and westward expansion.

▶ **Across the Continent**
Read a firsthand account of 1869 rail travel on this site.

▶ **Andrew J. Russell Collection**
A photo documentary of the Union Pacific Railroad.

▶ **Building the Central Pacific—A Narrative History**
The California State Archives offers this article about the Transcontinental Railroad.

▶ **Building the Transcontinental Railroad**
The Library of Congress presents historical documents pertaining to the Union Pacific Railroad.

▶ **California State Railroad Museum**
Learn about the era of the iron horse from the California State Railroad Museum.

▶ **Chinese Laborers in the West**
Find out about Chinese immigrant life in California.

▶ **Chinese-American Contribution to Transcontinental Railroad**
Many Chinese workers were hired to build the Transcontinental Railroad.

▶ **Diary of Judge A. N. Ferguson**
Read about the Transcontinental Railroad from the diary of a judge.

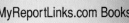
Report Links

The Internet sites described below can be accessed at
http://www.myreportlinks.com

▶**Golden Spike National Historic Site Utah**
A full-text online historical handbook about the building of a railroad.

▶**History of the Promontory Area**
You can read the interesting history of Promontory Summit, Utah, on this Web site.

▶**National Railroad Museum**
This is the virtual home to one of the most historic railroad collections in the country.

▶**New Perspectives on the West**
Biographies of important western Historical Figures.

▶**An Outline of American History**
View this online book on the transformation of a country.

▶**Pacific Railway Act**
View the Pacific Railway Act at this Library of Congress Web site.

▶**Personal Diary Account by Capt. John Charles Currier**
The National Park Service presents a historical narrative on the Transcontinental Railroad.

▶**Portraits of American Railroading**
Learn about American railroaders at this online Smithsonian National Portrait Gallery exhibition.

▶**Postal History of the First Transcontinental Railroad**
This online resource describes how the delivery of mail became easier with rail transportation.

▶**A Practical Plan for Building the Pacific Railroad**
Read Theodore Judah's plan for building the Transcontinental Railroad.

▶**Railroad Maps 1828–1900**
View historical railroad maps and surveys preserved by the Library of Congress.

▶**Railroad Vision**
A pictorial history of the railroads is available on this site.

▶**Research Papers**
Read the National Park Service's collection of railroad research papers.

▶**Stanford University: The Founding of the University**
Learn about one of the main investors of the railroad and his creation of a university.

▶**Today in History: May 10**
The construction of the Transcontinental Railroad finally comes to an end.

annexed—Seized by political action or conquest.

assassinated—Murdered for political reasons.

cholera—An intestinal infection caused by contaminated water or food.

entrepreneur—Person who organizes a new business venture.

gorge—A narrow pass through two sections of land that usually includes a steep cliff or canyon.

Great American Desert—Another phrase used to describe the Great Plains area of the United States. It is not truly a desert, but a large span of treeless grasslands.

Hell on Wheels—Wild, and out of control.

indentured—Contracted to work for another for a specific amount of time in return for payment of travel and basic living expenses.

inscribed—Written on or carved into a surface.

ironclad—A boat covered with armor that was widely used in the mid- to late-1800s.

isthmus—A narrow neck of land connecting two larger land areas.

malaria—An infectious disease caused by parasites carried by mosquitoes.

manifest destiny—The policy that extending rule over foreign countries is a necessary and moral duty.

manipulations—Actions that influence matters for one's own advantage, often deceitfully.

seceding—Formally withdrawing from membership in an organization or union.

Sierra Nevadas—A mountain range that spans the eastern portion of California to the western portion of Nevada.

tamp—To use a series of soft or medium hits to force something into place.

territory—A geographical area; a part of the United States not included within any state but organized with separate governing officials.

ultimatum—A final and absolute demand, often backed up by a threat.

yellow fever—A disease caused by a virus transmitted by a mosquito.

Chapter 1. Danger in the High Sierras

1. David Haward Bain, *Empire Express: Building the First Transcontinental Railroad* (New York: Viking, 1999), pp. 95–101.

2. Ibid., p. 97.

3. Ibid., p. 98.

4. Ibid., p. 100.

5. David C. Hanson, "The Fateful Journey of the Donner Party," *Virginia Western Community College,* 2003, <http://www.vw.vccs.edu/vwhansd/HIS121/Donner.html> (May 24, 2005).

6. "American Experience: the Transcontinental Railroad," *PBS Online,* 1999–2003, <http://www.pbs.org/wgbh/amex/tcrr/filmmore/pt.html> (May 24, 2003).

7. "People & Events: Asa Whitney (1791–1874) and Early Plans for a Transcontinental Railroad," *PBS Online,* 1999–2003, <http://www.pbs.org/wgbh/amex/tcrr/peopleevents/e_early.html> (May 24, 2005).

8. Bain, p. 9.

9. "People & Events: Asa Whitney (1791–1874) and Early Plans for a Transcontinental Railroad," *PBS Online,* <http://www.pbs.org/wgbh/amex/tcrr/peopleevents/e_early.html> (May 24, 2005).

10. Ibid.

11. Bain, p. 27.

12. "American West," *History on the Net, 2000,* <http://www.historyonthenet.com/American_West/great_american_desert.htm> (May 24, 2005).

13. "American Experience: the Transcontinental Railroad," *PBS Online,* 1999–2003, <http://www.pbs.org/wgbh/amex/tcrr/filmmore/pt.html> (May 24, 2005).

14. Thomas Jefferson, "To the Governor of Virginia (James Monroe) Washington, Nov. 24, 1801," *The Letters of Thomas Jefferson: 1743–1826,* 1994–2005, <http://odur.let.rug.nl/~usa/P/tj3/writings/brf/jefl142.htm> (May 24, 2005).

Chapter 2. Seeing the Possibilities

1. David Haward Bain, *Empire Express: Building the First Transcontinental Railroad* (New York: Viking, 1999), p. 26.

2. John O'Sullivan, "Annexation," *The United States Magazine and Democratic Review,* (July 1845), pp. 5–10.

3. KERA, "Manifest Destiny: an Introduction," *PBS Online,* n.d., <http://www.pbs.org/kera/usmexicanwar/dialogues/prelude/manifest/d2aeng.html> (May 24, 2005).

4. Ibid.

5. Michael Trinklein, "The Oregon Trail," 1997–2003, <http://www.isu.edu/%7Etrinmich/Introduction.html> (May 24, 2005).

6. "Riding The Overland Stage, 1861," *EyeWitness to History,* 1998, <http://www.eyewitnesstohistory.com/stage.htm> (May 24, 2005).

7. Ibid.

8. Mark Twain, *Roughing It,* as posted at Eye Witness to History, 1998, <http://www.eyewitnesstohistory.com/stage.htm> (May 24, 2005).

9. Ibid.

10. Stephen E. Ambrose, *Nothing Like It In the World: The Men Who Built the Transcontinental Railroad 1863–1869* (New York: Simon & Schuster, 2001), pp. 53–54.

11. Oliver Jensen, *The American Heritage History of Railroads in America* (New York: Bonanza Books, 1975), p. 29.

12. H.B. Latrobe, excerpt from a letter, from Daniel Van Winkle, *Old Bergen,* Chapter XXXII, published 1902, <http://www.cityofjerseycity.org/oldberg/chapter33.shtml> (May 24, 2005).

13. Jensen, p. 29.

14. David M. Stokes, "Railroads Blue & Gray," *National Railroad Historical Society,* 2000–05, <http://www.nrhs.com/spot/civilwar/> (May 24, 2005).

Chapter 3. Getting Started, 1860–1863

1. Stephen E. Ambrose, *Nothing Like It In the World: The Men Who Built the Transcontinental Railroad 1863–1869* (New York: Simon & Schuster, 2001), p. 30.

2. R.D. Monroe, Ph.D., "The Kansas-Nebraska Act and the Rise of the Republican Party, 1854–1856," *Abraham Lincoln Digitization Project,* 2000, <http://lincoln.lib.niu.edu/biography6text.html> (May 24, 2005).

3. "The Great Locomotive Chase," Oliver Jensen, *The American Heritage History of Railroads in America* (New York: Bonanza Books, 1975), pp. 74–77.

4. Ibid., p. 74.

5. Ibid., p. 76.

6. "American Experience: the Transcontinental Railroad," *PBS Online,* 1999–2003, <http://www.pbs.org/wgbh/amex/tcrr/filmmore/pt.html> (May 24, 2005).

Chapter 4. Building the Railroad, 1863–1869

1. David Haward Bain, *Empire Express: Building the First Transcontinental Railroad* (New York: Viking, 1999), p. 221.

2. Ibid., p. 238.

3. Ibid., p. 239.

4. Ibid., p. 240.

5. Stephen E. Ambrose, *Nothing Like It In the World: The Men Who Built the Transcontinental Railroad 1863–1869* (New York: Simon & Schuster, 2001), p. 160.

6. Bain, p. 317.

7. "People & Events: Nitroglycerin," *PBS Online,* 1999–2003, <http://www.pbs.org/wgbh/amex/tcrr/peopleevents/e_nitro.html> (May 24, 2005).

8. Bain, p. 321.

9. Ambrose, p. 177.

10. Ibid., pp. 177–178.

11. Bain, p. 265.

12. Ibid., p. 230.

13. "American Experience: the Transcontinental Railroad," *PBS Online,* 1999–2003, <http://www .pbs.org/wgbh/amex/tcrr/filmmore/pt.html> (May 24, 2005).

14. Oliver Jensen, *The American Heritage History of Railroads in America* (New York: Bonanza Books, 1975), p. 98.

15. Ambrose, pp. 359–360.

16. Ibid., p. 360.

Chapter 5. Supporters, Builders, and Profiteers

1. Cristalen, "Biographic Notes: Charles Crocker," *Inn-California,* n.d., <http://www.inn-california .com/Articles/biographic/ccrockerbio.html> (May 24, 2005).

2. Mary Alice McClure, "General Grenville M. Dodge," *Pottawattamie County (Iowa) Genealogy,* n.d., <http://www.rootsweb.com/~iapottaw/ Dodge.htm> (May 24, 2005).

3. "Historic Figures: Thomas Clark Durant (1820–1885)," *BBC,* n.d., <http://www.bbc.co .uk/history/historic_figures/durant_thomas_clark .shtml> (May 24, 2005).

4. The Rector and Visitors of the University of Virginia, "Ulysses Simpson Grant (1869–1877)," *Americanpresident.org,* 2003, <http://www .americanpresident.org/history/ulyssessgrant/> (May 24, 2005).

5. "Hopkins, Mark, Concise Encyclopedia Article," *Encyclopaedia Brittanica,* 2005, <http://www .britannica.com/ebc/article?tocId=9367341&query =Mark%20Twain&ct=gen1> (May 24, 2005).

6. Eric Howard, "Collis P. Huntington," as posted at *Diana's Genealogy Homepage,* 1932, <http://dgmweb.net/genealogy/7/NRoots/Bios/Bio-CPHuntington-Howard1932.shtml> (May 24, 2005).

7. R.D. Monroe, Ph.D., "Boyhood and Migration, 1815–1830," *Lincoln's Biography,* 2000, <http://lincoln.lib.niu.edu/biography1text.html> (May 24, 2005).

8. "George Pullman: Pullman Sleeping Car," *MIT School of Engineering,* April 2003, <http://web.mit.edu/invent/iow/pullman.html> (May 24, 2005).

Chapter 6. Tying the Eastern to the Western Sea

1. Stephen E. Ambrose, *Nothing Like It In the World: The Men Who Built the Transcontinental Railroad 1863–1869* (New York: Simon & Schuster, 2001), p. 252.

2. "American Experience: the Transcontinental Railroad," *PBS Online,* 1999–2003, <http://www.pbs.org/wgbh/amex/tcrr/filmmore/pt.html> (May 24, 2005).

3. Ambrose, p. 373.

4. "Durant's Big Scam," *PBS Online,* 1999–2003, <http://www.pbs.org/wgbh/amex/tcrr/sfeature/sf_scandals.html> (May 25, 2005).

5. "People and Events: Hell on Wheels," *PBS Online,* 1999–2003, <http://www.pbs.org/wgbh/amex/tcrr/peopleevents/e_hell.html> (May 25, 2005).

6. University of Northern Iowa, "Iowa Railway Guide," *Explorations in Iowa History Project,* 2003, <http://fp.uni.edu/iowahist/Frontier_Life/Railway _Guide/RailwayGuide.htm> (May 25, 2005).

7. Ambrose, p. 362.

8. "People & Events: The Impact of the Transcontinental Railroad," *PBS Online,* 1999–2003, <http://www.pbs.org/wgbh/amex/tcrr/peopleeven ts/e_impact.html> (May 25, 2005).

9. Ambrose, p. 20.

10. J.W. Conner, "John Chinaman, My Jo," *Conner's Irish Song Book,* 1868, as posted by *The Mudcat Cafe,* <http://www.mudcat.org/@displaysong .cfm?SongID=3237> (May 25, 2005).

11. "A Folk Version of the Ballad," *John Henry: The Steel Driving Man,* n.d., <http://www.ibiblio .org/john_henry/folk.html> (May 25, 2005).

Ambrose, Stephen E. *Nothing Like It In the World: The Men Who Built the Transcontinental Railroad 1863–1869*. New York: Simon & Schuster, 2001.

Bailer, Darice. *Last Rail: The Building of the First Transcontinental Railroad*. Norwalk, Conn.: Soundprints, 1996.

Blashfield, Jean F. *The Transcontinental Railroad*. Minneapolis: Compass Point Books, 2001.

Durbin, William. *My Name Is America: The Journal Of Sean Sullivan, A Transcontinental Railroad Worker*. New York: Scholastic, Inc., 1999.

Fraser, Mary Ann. *Ten Mile Day: And the Building of the Transcontinental Railroad*. New York: Henry Holt and Co., 1996.

Halpern, Monica. *Railroad Fever: Building the Transcontinental Railroad 1830–1870*. Washington, D.C.: National Geographic Children's Books, 2004.

Perl, Lila. *To the Golden Mountain: The Story of the Chinese who Built the Transcontinental Railroad*. New York: Benchmark Books, 2003.

Streissguth, Tom. *The Transcontinental Railroad*. San Diego, Calif.: Lucent Books, 2000.

Thompson, Linda. *The Transcontinental Railroad (The Expansion of America)*. Vero Beach, Fla.: Rourke Publishing, 2005.